JOBS FOR ROBOTS

Between Robocalypse and Robotopia

JASON SCHENKER

For my mother and father.

CONTENTS

6 JOBS FOR ROBOTS

SO HOT RIGHT NOW

Like Hansel in the movie *Zoolander*, robots and automation are "so hot right now." Books, articles, and television segments on automation, robotics, universal basic income, and the future of work are coming to dominate the *Zeitgeist* — the spirit of our time. People are becoming increasingly aware that automation and robots are going to be important — and unavoidable — parts of their working and non-working lives.

The Trend is Your Friend

Google Trends data in charts at the end of this chapter show just how hot these topics have become. In February 2017, when this book went to print, online searches for the terms "robots," "automation," "future of work," and "universal basic income" had increased dramatically, with "robots"[1] and "automation"[2] at the highest levels since 2007. Meanwhile, searches for the terms "future of work"[3] and "universal basic income"[4] were near all-time highs in 2016 and 2017.

Robocalypse and Robotopia

When people talk about robots and the future of work, they tend to reductively couch the outlook in one of two ways. At one end of the spectrum is the vision of Robocalypse: an apocalyptic future explicitly caused by robots, automation, and artificial intelligence. At the other end of the spectrum, is the vision of Robotopia: a heaven-on-earth future world of leisure, where all work is done for us by the machines.

While Robocalypse is reductively and often unnecessarily terrifying, Robotopia is pure kitsch. Both scenarios make for interesting movies (although Robocalypse films tend to be better and more compelling), but both of these polarized presentations of future existence are gross oversimplifications.

The most probable future outcome is likely to be somewhere between a Robocalypse and a Robotopia. There will be winners and losers. And having the proper frame of reference, level of preparedness, access to training and education, and access to job openings will be the critical determining factors of individual and societal success or failure.

The future is going to be more like the *Jetsons* than *The Terminator* or *Star Trek*. It will be different, but perhaps not exciting enough to be a blockbuster. And that's ok. After all, only documentaries have been made about the invention of ATMs and the industrial robots that factories use. Maybe ATM and robotic arm movie scripts have been written, but I doubt it. Most technology is seamlessly absorbed, which is likely to remain true in the future.

The Past and Future of Work

The philosopher George Santayana wrote that "those who do not remember the past are condemned to repeat it."[5] In the case of robots, automation, and the future of work, I believe that those who do not know their past are doomed to be overly fearful of it. There isn't a lot of demand on the lecture circuit to hear futurists talk about medieval European labor economics and surname etymology, but these topics present the most comforting examples to start with, when thinking about the future of work.

There is great value in taking a step back in time, in order to see the future more clearly. And this book presents past work changes in a way that contextualizes the advantages we have today, when facing the future of work in the automation age.

Look at it this way: Smith is the most common surname in the English language.[6] From 1500 BC until 1800 AD, blacksmith was one of the most common occupations throughout the medieval and early modern periods.[7] People were so attached to this profession that they took on the last name Smith. But, we know better now, than to pick a last name based on our professions.

After an analytical look at the past, we'll look at the present of work and recent trends that affect the near-term outlook for labor. Then, we will look ahead to the future. But jumping right into the future of work, robots, and automation is an issue. We need to start with the *history of work*, before we discuss the *future of work*. Let's start with the Smiths, Schmidts, and LeFebvres. We will also make time for the Millers and Weavers.

Robocalypse for *Some* Jobs

The future of work is likely to hold a mix of good and bad ramifications for jobs and the labor market. For some jobs, industries, and professions, the negative impact of automation will be profound and swift. Conversely, for other industries, the future of work will present more opportunities. And somewhere in between, will be many jobs and professions that see parts of their current core functions automated — in much the same way that computers have affected all jobs. The pace of technological change will be quicker, but the experience of having seen past labor market changes is on our side. I certainly would prefer to be a worker today, who has seen transitions of technology in various capacities and be faced with these challenges, rather than a blacksmith emerging from the middle ages.

The ancient Greeks spoke of life as a hearth with two vases on it. There was a vase of good and a vase of bad. There was never a case in which you could have *only good*. The choice was always between a *mix of good and bad* — or *only bad*. Similarly, there is no technological change from automation and robots that is likely to be purely good for the future of work. However, it's also my belief, that there is no outcome that is purely bad either.

Robotopia and In-Hand Retail

Smartphones are store fronts in your hand, and e-commerce has created a world of in-hand retail that is likely to accelerate. The self-service movement is real, and only highly customized, automated workers can get our supply chain there. This is one of the biggest upside opportunities for Robotopia, which I discuss at length in Chapter 5.

If the supply chain can keep up with in-hand retail demands, then our access to goods and services — as well as choice of goods — will increase. In-hand retail presents some risks to retail jobs, but people's time — their most valuable asset — may be liberated from long lines. Automated transport is also likely to increase mobility options for individuals, while also freeing people's time.

In sum, there are three big plusses that robots and automation bring to the world:

They free your time.
They free your movement.
They increase your access to goods and services.

This is the stuff of the *Declaration of Independence*: Life, Liberty, and the Pursuit of Happiness.[8] And yet, it is the U.S. government's own unbalanced books that could end the upside potential for the automation and robotics party, before it even starts.

The Need for Entitlement Reform

Medicare, Medicaid, and Social Security unfunded obligations total up to $200 trillion. In Chapter 6, I present the risks to the overall labor market from unreformed entitlements that stem from a rising national debt, changes in the population pyramid, and expected costs of future unfunded obligations. While there are significant upside opportunities from robotics and automation, a lack of entitlement reform threatens to upend the cart. The pathway to hell may be paved with good intentions, but the road to serfdom is apparently paved with unfunded entitlements.

The Folly of Universal Basic Income (UBI)

One interesting part of both the Robocalypse and Robotopia narratives is the concept of universal basic income (UBI), which is the notion that everyone — working or not — should receive income from the government. Whether the robots take all the jobs and impoverish the world, or if they enrich the world and make work superfluous, the government gives everyone money.

There are a number of problems with this plan that I address in Chapter 7. The biggest problem is a direct follow-on from my discussion in Chapter 6 about entitlements and the U.S. national debt: we simply cannot afford a UBI plan. Aside from the budgetary concerns, there are four big reasons to avoid implementing such a UBI plan: inflation, higher tax rates, disincentives for future economic and technological development, and societal risks that stem from having a completely unoccupied populace. If idle hands are the work of the devil, UBI could be a great recruiting tool.

In-Hand Classroom

The greatest defense against a future Robocalypse is an educated and adaptive workforce. We need to bridge education and skills gaps, and the in-hand classroom is a critical tool to help people survive and thrive during the coming robotic and automation changes to the labor market. Fortunately, access to online courses, certifications, professional designations, Bachelor's degrees, and Master's degrees has rapidly expanded. And the future of online education is likely to expand and accelerate further. This is the main subject of Chapter 8.

In-Hand Labor Market

Prior to the industrial revolution, your career options would have been limited to your village, and thereafter, your options would have been limited to ads in the paper. Now, however, 20 million job listings can be viewed in your hand instantly. This in-hand labor market increases access to job opportunities. In a world of increased automation, our ability to remain intellectually nimble is paired with the need to rapidly match skills with available opportunities. For this, the in-hand labor market, which has seen significant developments in the internet age, will become an even more critical component of success in the automation age.

Be Prepared to Robot-Proof Your Career

After examining the downside risks, upside opportunities, and critical conditions to ensure the economy and society will benefit from automation and robotics, I present some recommendations for individuals reading this book. Workers need to seek out evergreen professional opportunities wherever they are, as well as embrace education and skill-building opportunities. Without more education and skills — and a willingness and preparedness to adapt at a more rapid pace — you will be left behind. Trucking, transport, and retail could become professional wastelands, while healthcare, automation, information technology, and project management are likely to be professional promised lands.

Up Next: Why I Wrote This Book

In the next chapter, I share the impetus that drove me to write this book, which is a mix of data, statistics, economics, history, and the future of work. But first, let's see those Google Trends graphs showing robots and automation are "so hot right now."

Figure 0-1: U.S. Google Trends for Robots at 2007 Levels[9]

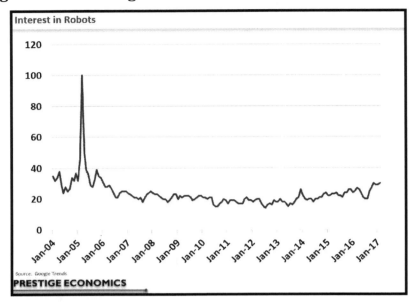

Figure 0-2: U.S. Google Trends Automation at 2007 Levels[10]

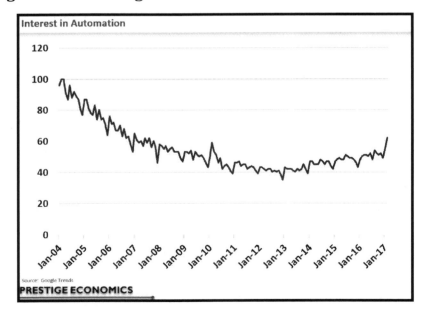

Figure 0-3: U.S. Google Trends Future of Work Near High[11]

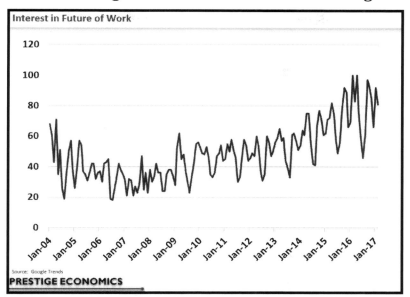

Figure 0-4: U.S. Google Trends Universal Basic Income High[12]

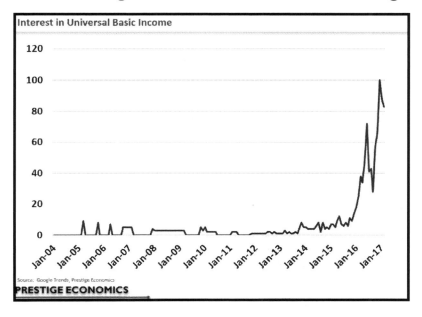

CHAPTER 1

WHY I WROTE THIS BOOK FOR YOU

Everyone is talking about robots. But no one is talking about the most important issues that will determine whether robots will make our lives better or worse: entitlement reform, bridging the education gap, and applying an informed historical perspective to future challenges.

There is a tendency in the debate about automation and robots that lends itself to reductively presenting the future as dystopian or utopian — as Robocalypse or Robotopia. And yet, the most critical drivers are fundamental; the future depends on how we manage labor, education, and tax policies.

This debate has been hyped up because it affects everyone, and the future of work is important. Plus, stories of a dystopian Robocalypse, in which robots and automation take all the jobs and threaten all of society, resonate with anyone who has ever seen a science-fiction movie like *The Terminator*. As some in journalism like to say: if it bleeds, it leads. And nothing bleeds quite like the prospects of a Robocalypse.

It is important to examine both the downside risks and upside opportunities presented by automation, robotics, and artificial intelligence. After all, both upside and downside risks exist. But I primarily wrote this book to raise awareness about the importance of bridging critical gaps in the way we talk about the future of work, the importance of education, and the critical need for entitlement reform, so that individuals and society can reap the benefits from the upside potential presented by a Robotopia — and to mitigate the downside risks of a Robocalypse.

This Book is for Everyone

When futurists, analysts, and policymakers speak about the future of work, it affects everyone. Everyone. That includes you, your children, your grandchildren, your great-grandchildren, and anyone you and they know, have known, and ever will know. So, it's kind of a big deal. Like the debate about the future of work itself, this book is for everyone.

A Need for Context

Taking a nuanced and contextualized look at a subject that is often sledgehammered by overly simplistic (but often fascinating) Robocalyptic visions is important to advancing a debate over the issues that matter. The self-service revolution is real, and therein lies both the cure and the cause of risk. We want more, now. The Frankfurt School, which was a group of philosophers in pre-World War II Germany, referred to this concept as "commodity fetishism." Basically, above almost all else, people love to buy things. Today, our desire for in-hand retail is part of our desire for in-hand everything: business, class-room, office, labor market, and love life.

While Tinder is unlikely to improve your future professional prospects, MOOCs and online job boards are.

In the late 1990s, there were postcards with pictures of cell phones that said "Home is where my phone is." That was not true in the 1990s, but it is closer to being true today. In fact, you could also add in 2017 that, "My mall, my classroom, my office, and my career search are where my phone is." That dynamic of in-hand everything will continue to propel our economy and professional lives forward, even if jobs appear to be threatened.

Futurists are the Future

Speaking in 2009, Hal Varian, chief economist at Google, praised "statistician" as being "the sexy job in the next 10 years."[1] But that 10 year period is almost over.

Applied statistics and econometrics have been critical for data analysis. And statisticians have made tremendous contributions to analyzing big data in most of the past decade. As our ability to manage and analyze increasingly larger sets of data has improved, so has our ability to analyze short-term dynamics in weather, financial markets, and customer behavior.

But now, there is a growing need for a new type of analyst. Longer-term analysis is where improvements and future developments are needed. This is where futurists come in. And the field of futurists is growing. "Futurist" is likely to be the sexy job of the next 10 years.

Et Moi?

I have been a professional business economist since 2004, and this book is the culmination of my transition from economist to financial market futurist. My client needs in recent years have propelled my analysis further and further into the future. And the transition to futurist has not been easy. It is the key reason I founded the Futurist Institute of America in October 2016 to help economists and analysts build their longer-term analytical skills.

But I am unique among financial market futurists, as I am the only futurist with a track record of forecasting accurately. In fact, Bloomberg News has recognized me as one of the top forecasters in the world for the accuracy of my economic and financial market forecasts as the President of Prestige Economics.

My track record since 2011 has included top rankings for my forecast accuracy across 35 different categories, including accuracy rankings as #1 in world in 20 different categories. Simply put, there is no other futurist in world with this level of accuracy in predicting the future. It's my job to predict the future, and I want to share it with you.

As for my academic background, I hold a Bachelor's degree, four professional certifications, and three Master's degrees. The most relevant for this book is my Master's in Applied Economics, which is often labeled as econometrics, and focused on the application of economic analysis to statistics. I finished that degree in 2003, which means that I finished my degree in a statistically-related subject area five years before an exec at Google said it would be sexy. Apparently, I was a budding futurist early on!

Figure 1-1: Prestige Economics Rankings[3]

Bloomberg News Top Rankings for Prestige Economics in 35 Different Categories Since 2011

Top Energy Rankings

#1 WTI Crude Oil Price Forecaster in the World
#1 Brent Crude Oil Price Forecaster in the World
#1 Henry Hub Natural Gas Price Forecaster in the World

Top Metals Rankings

#1 Gold Price Forecaster in the World
#1 Platinum Price Forecaster in the World
#1 Industrial Metals Price Forecaster in the World
#1 Copper Price Forecaster in the World
#1 Nickel Price Forecaster in the World
#1 Tin Price Forecaster in the World
#1 Zinc Price Forecaster in the World
#2 Precious Metals Price Forecaster in the World
#2 Silver Price Forecaster in the World
#2 Palladium Price Forecaster in the World
#2 Aluminum Price Forecaster in the World
#2 Lead Price Forecaster in the World
#2 Iron Ore Forecaster in the World

Prestige Economics Has Been Top Ranked Based on Forecasts Produced for Every Quarter Since Being Founded in 2009

PRESTIGE ECONOMICS

Top Currency Rankings

#1 Euro Forecaster in the World
#1 British Pound Forecaster in the World
#1 Swiss Franc Forecaster in the World
#1 Brazilian Real Forecaster in the World
#4 Japanese Yen Forecaster in the World
#5 Major Currency Forecaster in the World
#5 Australian Dollar Forecaster in the World
#1 EURCHF Forecaster in the World
#2 EURJPY Forecaster in the World
#2 EURGBP Forecaster in the World
#2 EURRUB Forecaster in the World

Top Agricultural Rankings

#1 Coffee Price Forecaster in the World
#1 Cotton Price Forecaster in the World
#1 Sugar Price Forecaster in the World
#1 Soybean Price Forecaster in the World

Top Economic Rankings

#1 Non-Farm Payroll Forecaster in the World
#2 Unemployment Rate Forecaster in the World
#3 Durable Goods Orders Forecaster in the World
#7 ISM Manufacturing Index Forecaster in the World

Source: Bloomberg News

Although I am a futurist, I am not a Singulatarian,[2] who believes we will all become cyborgs, merging carbon-based and silicon-based intellect. Given my background in economics, I believe people and companies will respond to incentives, and that they will leverage the opportunities they have.

Technological evolution is changing rapidly, and I believe the human experience will allow us to adapt without becoming part of a technological or political Borg. I have more faith in humans than that. We have faced bigger professional challenges. To see how big those changes were, just grab any phonebook — after reading the next chapter.

CHAPTER 2

THE PAST OF WORK: WHAT'S IN A NAME?

The most common family name in the English language is Smith.[1] But how many Smiths do you know working in a blacksmith's forge? My guess: zero. In fact, to see a blacksmith today, you probably need to go to a living museum, like Plimoth Plantation or Colonial Williamsburg, as in Figure 2-1. You could probably also find a blacksmith in action at a Renaissance Faire. Of course, those people are essentially performers, whose surnames are unlikely to be Smith. The truth is that many people with the surname Smith have likely never even seen a blacksmith at work.

Smiths, as a profession, trace their roots back to the first iron age blacksmiths around 1500 B.C.[2] In England, occupational surnames like Smith were solidified in the twelfth century,[3] and this occupation continued to flourish until the late 1800s when railways ushered in the age of iron and steel.[4] At that point, "the Industrial Age made small enterprises all but obsolete....[since] the railroads had linked the country and hardware was manufactured at plants and sold in hardware stores."[5] At that time, Smiths ceased being smiths.

Figure 2-1: Blacksmith Working in a Forge[6]

A similar experience swept across Europe. In Germany, Schmidt is one of the most common surnames, and in France, LeFebvre is very common. Schmidts and LeFebvres were also blacksmiths — and they also saw their profession vanish.

Now, imagine what that kind of upheaval in the professions was like? People understand today that the workforce changes rapidly, and that education and skill requirements are an ever-evolving situation. But in the late 1800s, these kinds of changes were unprecedented.

While we are concerned about automation, robots, and artificial intelligence, consider for a moment that blacksmiths existed as a successful profession for almost 3,400 years. And within a span of about a century, that entire industry completely vanished. In the twelfth century — almost 800 years before the demise of the blacksmithing industry — people chose their surnames to be Smith. They chose to be forever identified by this profession, which they likely presumed would forever exist, which — given that the profession had already been around for over 2,600 years — did not seem like an unreasonable expectation.

Of course, blacksmith was not the only profession disrupted (to use a modern buzzword) by the industrial revolution. Millers, weavers, and others saw their professions decimated. Today, mills exist as museums where you can watch grains be ground between rotating stones. It's great sightseeing, as you can see in Figure 2-2! But only tour guides actually work there now.

Figure 2-2: Pre-industrial Mills are now Museums[7]

Changing and Unchanging Names

The occupational surnames Smith, Miller, and Weaver conjure an image of medieval villages that were completely upended after centuries or millennia. These occupational names had a staying power, however. According to name historian J.R. Dolan, occupational surnames "stayed with the individual to a much greater extent" than surnames derived from nicknames, place names, and relationship names.[8] This was due to the economics of skill and goods accumulation in trades that kept families in occupations for generations.

Can you imagine a world in which you not only had the same job and occupation for your entire life, but that it intergenerationally impacted your whole family? Sure, some family businesses are like this, but not to the extent that people change their last name to reflect their new jobs.

Tavern Keepers and Futurists

My last name, Schenker, is a German occupational name that means "tavern keeper." But no one in my family is a tavern keeper. Sure, it might be fun to own a bar on 6th Street in Austin, but generally speaking, none of us aspires to be tavern keepers. Neither they, nor I, bemoan the loss of that career. In fact, this vestige of a family business that spanned many generations in a village in Europe was so far forgotten in my family memory, that until I studied German in college, no one in my family even knew what the name meant. No one. Not me. Not my parents. Not my grandparents. And my grandchildren may feel the same way. They may even live at a time when my career as a futurist is not something anyone does or would like to do.

Imagine that: a future without futurists. I am certainly not running out to change my name to Jason Futurist, and I wager that my wife isn't changing her name to Ashley Project Manager any time soon either.

I do not think there are many people who would choose an occupational surname today, believing it would have any durability over time. After all, according to data from the U.S. Bureau of Labor Statistics, between 35 and 40 percent of all employees change jobs every single year. In the twelve months through December 2016, about 38 percent of workers experienced turnover, with 60.1 million workers separated and 62.5 million workers hired.[9]

The Past Future of Work

If I was writing a book about the future of work back in medieval times, they would have burned me at the stake. No one would have believed that blacksmiths would have been replaced by machines in factories. They most certainly would not have believed that people could work in offices on computers that did some of the thinking for them. But even if they had believed that, they would not have believed that people could have done this remotely and with their office in their hand. Yup, I definitely would have been burned at the stake for that one.

While people worked in mills and forges for thousands of years, we have worked in offices for a little more than a century. But we know that can change — and that it is likely to change. Manufacturers have seen jobs go overseas or decline during the first wave of industrial automation. The future of work could see some of those jobs come back to the United States, but those jobs will likely be jobs for robots. This is something I discussed in my last book, *Electing Recession*.

Future Adaptation: Quicker But Expected
Workforce changes are likely to come more rapidly with automation and robots than in the past. But we need to understand that the magnitude and unexpected nature of workforce upheaval during the industrial revolution was likely greater than anything we will experience. After all, there were no online job boards, no online education opportunities, and much more limited mobility. Most importantly, we are more aware of the economic world around us today than ever before — and certainly much more than villagers in the late 1800s. This contributes to the greatest advantage we have over our ancestors: we expect change.

Jobs are going to change, but we are not as tied to them as our ancestors were tied to other professions in history. The idea of co-working spaces, remote working environments, more individualised work, and the shift from W-2 employees to 1099 contract workers has already begun. But these changes are less tectonic than those experienced at the onset of the industrial revolution.

Figure 2-3: The Past of Work.[10]

The jobs of tomorrow will look much more like the jobs of today, compared to the changes experienced when jobs transitioned from village-oriented and guild-centric occupations, to industrial or academic careers.

The change now isn't about leaving behind three thousands years of an ancestral profession; the change now is about adapting to the new intellectual work we will need to do. Of course, the move to an intellectual economy is already happening. Now, with automation and robotics, there's going to be an acceleration.

Labor Museums of Tomorrow

In my book *Recession-Proof,* I examined the notion of offices as an important part of our lives that would likely become obsolete in the not too distant future. We need to be aware that the jobs we do today could be artifacts tomorrow. After all, being a miller was an occupation, but now mills just make lovely museums, like the one in Figure 2-3. This long ago became a job for robots, when electricity and the industrial revolution made this job redundant. Is it possible then, that an office, like the one in Figure 2-4, could be a museum tomorrow? It could be. After all, traditional office space is already at risk.

From 2007 to 2009, I worked at McKinsey & Company, which is generally considered to be a leading global consulting firm. Even in 2007, most consultants did not have individual offices; the company operated with flexspace and remote working. And that was 10 years ago! Today, many companies have similar working structures. The in-hand office is ascending.

This is such a critical issue, that some of my institutional investor clients in New York City recently stressed their concerns about the potential impact of FinTech disruption and Roboadvising on New York City commercial real estate. The rise of passive asset management and the impact on traditional financial services is something I will discuss in Chapter 4. These dynamics reduce employment needs in financial services, and as a knock-on effect, fewer people need offices because economies of scale are more easily achieved with automation.

Figure 2-4: The Future Past of Work.[11]

Universal Basic Income

When we get to Chapter 7 on universal basic income, we will examine the need for adaptation in the face of technological unemployment. For now, I leave you to ponder a question: if governments had granted universal basic income to smiths and millers at the dawn of the industrial age, because of unexpected tectonic shifts in the labor market that were unprecedented before or since, what would Smiths and Millers be doing now?

.

CHAPTER 3

THE PRESENT OF WORK

Before we get to the chapter about Robocalypse, let's examine some information about the current state of the U.S. labor market and workforce, how it has developed in recent years, and what that says about critical drivers of growth and jobs in the coming decade.

This isn't a chapter about all of the evil technological changes that could lead to a Robocalypse, and it isn't a chapter about the benefits of a Robotopia. It is a snapshot of current economic and labor market conditions, as well as the current expectations for those held by myself, the Bureau of Labor Statistics (BLS), and others.

First, we will look at the historical trend of occupations in the U.S. labor force. Then, we will examine where robots, automation, and artificial intelligence are likely to be most — and least — impactful. Finally, we will look at some of the forecasts from the BLS for job growth and wages.

Figure 3-1: Employment in Agriculture and Other Areas[1]

Distribution of Labor Force by Sector in the United States, 1840-2010

Source: NBER, FRED, World Bank, Prestige Economics

PRESTIGE ECONOMICS

Farmpocalypse

Beyond the trades of medieval life that I discussed in the last chapter, another profession that has been pushed to the edge of oblivion by technology is agriculture. In 1840, almost two-thirds of the U.S. population was comprised of farmers. Today, that number is less than 2 percent.

You can see the sharp decline in agricultural jobs (as a percent of the total U.S. labor force) in Figure 3-1. You can also see that manufacturing jobs (as a percent of the total U.S. labor force) rose from 1840 until they peaked in 1920.[2] As a percent of the workforce, manufacturing has been in decline ever since.

Manufacturing Jobs

Manufacturing jobs have declined in absolute terms, and as a percent of the U.S. labor force, at the same time that automation impacted manufacturing. Of course, manufacturing has also been subject to a high degree of outsourcing. Nevertheless, the absolute number of U.S. manufacturing jobs peaked in 1979, and has generally fallen since (Figure 3-2).[3]

Politicians talk about creating and on-shoring manufacturing jobs that have gone abroad. But the only manufacturing jobs that are likely to be created domestically in large numbers are jobs for robots. Automation is likely to continue in manufacturing, and jobs that come onshore could be a manifestation of automatable jobs that have become expensive and labor intensive overseas.

Figure 3-2: Employees in Manufacturing[4]

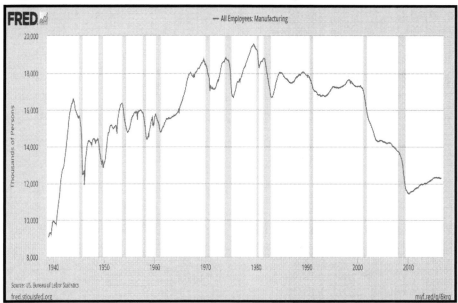

I have been to a number of U.S. factories that were highly automated. But even though these factories were high-tech, it was often the case, that some of the work was still being done by hand. This was usually a function of limited production runs, a need to manually assemble something small that would be wildly expensive to automate, and/or the demand for the goods was so high that wide profit margins justified manual assembly. But those cases for manufacturing were the exception, not the rule

Beyond Manufacturing

In addition to the decline of manufacturing jobs, the top non-manufacturing jobs have also changed significantly in recent decades. In just 36 years, the most common jobs in most states changed dramatically. In Figure 3-3, you can see that "secretary" was the most common occupation in 1978, by number of states (#1 in 21 states).[5] By contrast, Figure 3-4 shows that by 2014, "truck driver" had become the most common occupation, by number of states (#1 in 29 states).[6] Meanwhile, secretary was the most common job category in only five states by 2014. Of course, today, even the job title "secretary" has become an anachronism. This job description is used much less frequently now, and it has become less preferable to "administrative assistant," because computers have allowed us to become our own secretaries. We write our own letters (as emails), keep our own calendars (online), and manage our own contact lists (using LinkedIn). With automation, more change is coming. Truck driver is not likely to be the top occupation by number of states in 36 years. But, I wonder, will the actual name of the job itself also have fallen out of favor, as it has for secretary? Will the very concept of a truck driver be an anachronism? The odds look good.

Figure 3-3: Most Common Jobs by State — 1978[7]

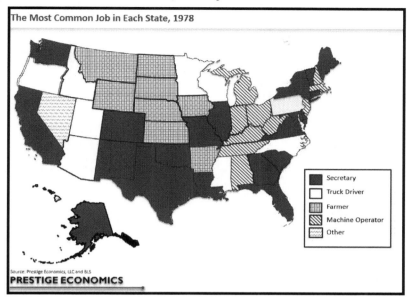

Figure 3-4: Most Common Jobs by State — 2014[8]

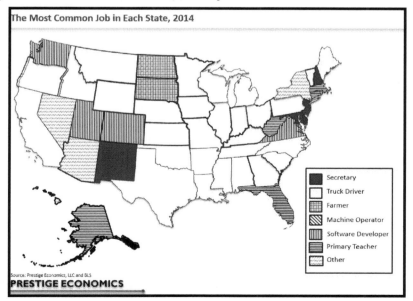

Productivity

Productivity is a measure of how much you get from each worker, and higher levels of productivity indicate more output per worker. There are two levers employers can use to achieve higher levels of worker productivity: capital and technology. This will drive future changes in the composition of the labor force.

In the past, productivity gains contributed to higher growth rates with the advent of the steam engine, early robotics, and IT. Based on research from the McKinsey Global Institute, the technological developments in Figure 3-5, added annual productivity growth of +0.3%, +0.4%, and +0.6 percent, respectively.[9]

Figure 3-5: Productivity Contributions from Technology[10]

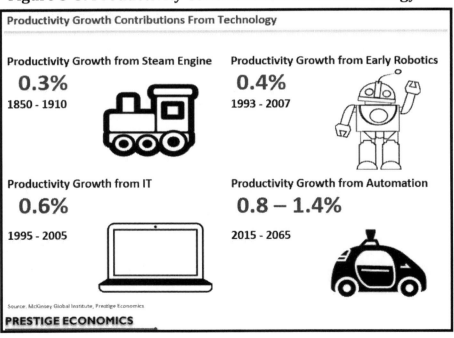

Productivity Growth Contributions From Technology

Productivity Growth from Steam Engine
0.3%
1850 - 1910

Productivity Growth from Early Robotics
0.4%
1993 - 2007

Productivity Growth from IT
0.6%
1995 - 2005

Productivity Growth from Automation
0.8 – 1.4%
2015 - 2065

Source: McKinsey Global Institute, Prestige Economics

PRESTIGE ECONOMICS

Looking Ahead

For the future impact of automation, the McKinsey Global Institute expects annual productivity gains of +0.8% to +1.4% for the 50 years through 2065.[11] That is a very long stretch, with very high expected productivity contributions. While that forecasted trend of productivity growth might be too long or too high, it is likely to be directionally correct. Automation will drive productivity — and growth — higher.

Capital, Labor, and Automation

When economists discuss the factors that drive growth, they tend to discuss the growth model of Nobel Prize winner Robert Solow.[12] The Solow growth model depicts the production function in an economy. In other words, it is a framework for showing how growth happens in an economy. It's quite simple really, since there are only three inputs that matter: capital (K), labor (L), and technology (A). For those of you who like economic formulas, the equation for the Solow growth model is typically written as follows:

$$Y = F(K,L,A)$$

This just means that production changes (Y) are a function (F) of K, L, and A. Although A represents technology in this equation, I would argue that in the future the A in this equation is likely to increasingly represent automation. And productivity gains will come, as robots are increasingly leveraged to perform a number of tasks.

Labor Advantages

Robots have traditionally performed rigid roles, where no logic has been required. However, robots are likely to expand their reach of logic and adaptability to quasi-structured situations in the medium term. Figure 3-6 shows a framework developed by Boston Consulting Group that compares robot labor advantages with human labor advantages. It also shows where robot skills are likely to develop next.

Robots' ability to act independently, develop their own logic, and perform tasks in unstructured environments is likely to be much further in the future. Even if robots could be taught these skills, there may not be a positive ROI to substitute robots for humans, since humans are likely to perform such tasks better than a bot.

Figure 3-6: BCG Framework of Labor Advantages[13]

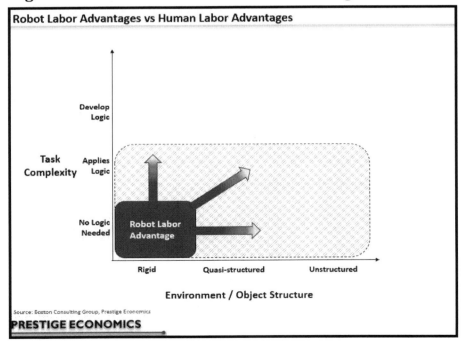

Robot Labor Advantages vs Human Labor Advantages

Develop Logic

Task Complexity — Applies Logic

No Logic Needed — Robot Labor Advantage

Rigid — Quasi-structured — Unstructured

Environment / Object Structure

Source: Boston Consulting Group, Prestige Economics

PRESTIGE ECONOMICS

Figure 3-7: Probability of Job Losses from Computers[14]

Probability of Losses Due to Computerization

JOB	PROBABILITY
Telemarketers	99%
Accountants/Auditors	94%
Retail Salespersons	92%
Technical Writers	89%
Real Estate Sales Agents	86%
Word Processors/Typists	81%
Machinists	65%
Commercial Pilots	55%
Economists	43%
Health Technologists	40%
Actors	37%
Firefighters	17%
Editors	6%
Chemical Engineers	2%
Clergy	0.8%
Athletic Trainers	0.7%
Dentists	0.4%
Recreational Therapists	0.3%

Source: Prestige Economics, The Economist, "The Future of Employment: How Susceptible are Jobs to Computerisation?" by C. Frey and M. Osborne (2013)

PRESTIGE ECONOMICS

Human Contact

There is a wide range of industry exposures as to how computerization and automation could eliminate jobs, which you can see in Figure 3-7. The jobs facing the highest probability of losses from computerization either have low education and skill requirements, or there is a formulaic nature of their work, which could be codified in a way that allows for automation.

Professions with significantly higher degrees of human contact, are likely to remain evergreen, be impervious to job losses, and even be exposed to further professional expansions. Let's look at a few examples of how occupations in this table could be impacted by increased automation and computerization.

Telemarketers

I have been receiving automated telemarketer calls for years. These so-called robocalls are not robots per se. They are just a computer program, designed and programmed to call you to sell and market goods or services. As you have likely experienced, robocalling telemarketers can be just as annoying as a real person. And the automated program does not get tired, discouraged, or insulted. Plus, a robocalling campaign is much cheaper to implement than a human telemarketing campaign, which is why, unfortunately, I expect robocalling will increase.

Accountants

Unlike telemarketing, accounting is a high-education and high-skill job. But some of the work, especially audits, are predicated on collecting and analyzing large amounts of data, and then applying a very specific and strict set of rules to the data. Data collection and rules-based analysis can be automated. For some stores, this is already going on. Real-time inventory management at retailers has increased, and with the advent of the LoweBot in Figure 5-2 in Chapter 5, you can see how audits will change.

Recreational Therapist and Athletic Trainer

Jobs with a personal touch cannot be easily replaced. For example, Brookstone (a high-tech retailer) has sold massage chairs for decades. But, massage therapists have not gone out of business. Similarly, athletic trainers are still around, despite countless hours of workout videos and in-home equipment. The reason for both is simple: you need a human guide and a human touch to get things done. Sometimes, a non-human substitute just will not do.

Overall Most Common U.S. Occupations

A depiction of the most common occupations nationally in the private sector can be seen in Figure 3-8. In a world of increasing automation, a number of these professions are at significant risk. Retail salespersons, cashiers, freight, stock, and hand material mover laborers, stock clerks and order fillers, as well as truck drivers, are exposed.

Fortunately, there is a growing need for other jobs in the U.S. economy. At the top of the list are professions that can help address the aging American populace. As such, this list is likely to change over time to reflect more healthcare jobs, as well as fewer jobs that could be automated out of existence.

Figure 3-8: Most Common U.S. Jobs[15]

Most Common Jobs in America	
JOB	**# EMPLOYED**
Retail Salespersons	4,155,190
Cashiers	3,354,170
Office Clerks	2,789,590
Food Preperation/Service Workers	2,692,170
Registered Nurses	2,751,000
Waiters	2,244,480
Customer Service Reps	2,146,120
Janitors and Cleaners	2,058,610
Freight, Stock, and Hand Material Mover Laborers	2,024,180
Secretaries and Administrative Assistants	1,841,020
Stock Clerks and Order Fillers	1,795,970
General and Operation Managers	1,708,080
Bookkeeping, Accounting, and Auditing Clerks	1,657,250
Elementary School Teachers	1,485,600
Truck Drivers	1,466,740

Source: BLS, Prestige Economics, Ranker.com

PRESTIGE ECONOMICS

Figure 3-9: Growth by Major Industry Sectors[16]

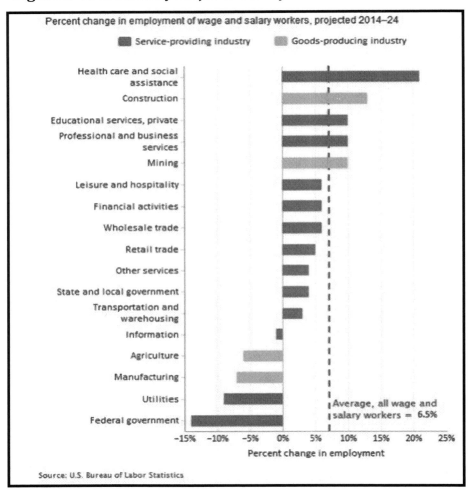

Percent change in employment of wage and salary workers, projected 2014–24

■ Service-providing industry   ■ Goods-producing industry

Source: U.S. Bureau of Labor Statistics

As you can see in Figure 3-9, the U.S. Bureau of Labor Statistics (BLS) expects that service sector jobs will remain the most critical sources of job creation through 2024. Healthcare tops the list by a wide margin. Construction and mining are the only two goods-producing sectors expected to grow through 2024.

The Most New Jobs by Occupation

Within the service sector, healthcare jobs dominate the BLS forecasts for the highest number of new jobs that are likely to be created through 2024. Personal care aides, registered nurses, and home health aides are the top three jobs in Figure 3-10. This reflects, in part, the needs of an aging American population.

The highest occupation category not in the health care space was food service workers. In recent years, there has been a mantra that *restaurants are the new retail*. Based on the need for food preparation/service workers and cooks, restaurants will remain critical areas of growth, even as e-commerce accelerates and more retail purchases happen online.

Figure 3-10: Greatest Number of New Jobs by Occupation[17]

Most New Jobs

OCCUPATION	NUMBER OF NEW JOBS (PROJECTED), 2014-24	2015 MEDIAN ANNUAL PAY
Personal Care Aides	458,100	$20,980
Registered Nurses	439,300	$67,490
Home Health Aides	348,400	$21,920
Food Preparation/Service Workers	343,500	$18,910
Retail Salespersons	314,200	$21,780
Nursing Assistants	262,000	$25,710
Customer Service Reps	252,900	$31,720
Cooks	158,900	$23,100
General/Operations Managers	151,100	$97,730
Construction Laborers	147,400	$31,910
Accountants/Auditors	142,400	$67,190
Medical Assistants	138,900	$30,590
Janitors/Cleaners	136,300	$23,440
Software Developers	135,300	$98,260
Laborers	125,100	$25,010
Administrative Support Workers	121,200	$52,630
Computer Systems Analysts	118,600	$85,800
Licensed Practical/Vocational Nurses	117,300	$43,170
Housekeepers	111,700	$20,740
Medical Secretaries	108,200	$33,040

Source: Bureau of Labor Statistics, Prestige Economics.

PRESTIGE ECONOMICS

Fastest-Growth Jobs by Occupation

Healthcare also dominates the occupation league tables for the fastest growth rates through 2024, according to the Bureau of Labor Statistics.

In Figure 3-11, you can see the 20 fastest-growing occupations in the United States, as forecasted by the BLS. Of the 20 fastest growth jobs, 13 are in health related fields. And healthcare jobs comprise six of the top 10 fastest-growing jobs, based on compensation. In other words, healthcare jobs are growing quickly. And many of them pay well.

Figure 3-11: Jobs with the Fastest Growth Rates[18]

Fastest Growing Jobs

OCCUPATION	GROWTH RATE, 2014-24	2015 MEDIAN ANNUAL PAY
Wind Turbine Service Technicians	108%	$51,050
Occupational Therapy Assistants	43%	$57,870
Physical Therapist Assistants	41%	$55,170
Physical Therapist Aides	39%	$25,120
Home Health Aides	38%	$21,920
Commercial Drivers	37%	$50,470
Nurse Practitioners	35%	$98,190
Physical Therapists	34%	$84,020
Statisticians	34%	$80,110
Ambulance Drivers and Attendants	33%	$23,740
Occupational Therapy Aides	31%	$27,800
Physician Assistants	30%	$98,180
Operations Research Analysts	30%	$78,630
Personal Financial Advisors	30%	$89,160
Cartographers and Photogrammetrists	29%	$61,880
Genetic Counselors	29%	$72,090
Interpreters and Translators	29%	$44,190
Audiologists	29%	$74,890
Hearing Aid Specialists	27%	$49,600
Optometrists	27%	$103,900

Source: Bureau of Labor Statistics, Prestige Economics.

PRESTIGE ECONOMICS

Highest-Paying Jobs by Occupation

Healthcare also dominates the league table for jobs with the highest median annual pay in the Untied States, according to the Bureau of Labor Statistics.

Healthcare accounts for 13 of the 14 highest-paying jobs by median annual pay in the United States, including 9 of the top 10. The BLS category "chief executive" is the only other occupation to break the top ten, and it comes in last at number 10. Of course, the downside to these top-paying medical occupations is the duration of schooling and training required for college, medical school, residency, and potential fellowships.

Figure 3-12: Jobs with the Highest Median Annual Pay[19]

OCCUPATION	2015 MEDIAN ANNUAL PAY
Physicians/Surgeons	$187,200
Surgeons	$187,200
Oral/Maxillofacial surgeons	$187,200
Internists/General	$187,200
Obstetricians/Gynecologists	$187,200
Psychiatrists	$187,200
Orthodontists	$187,200
Anesthesiologists	$187,200
Family/General Practitioners	$184,390
Chief Executives	$175,110
Dentists/All Other Specialists	$171,000
Pediatricians/General	$170,300
Nurse Anesthetists	$157,140
Dentists/General	$152,700
Architectural/Engineering Managers	$132,800
Computer/Information Systems Managers	$131,600
Petroleum Engineers	$129,990
Marketing Managers	$128,750
Judges/Magistrates	$126,930
Air Traffic Controllers	$122,950

Highest Paying Jobs

Source: Bureau of Labor Statistics, Prestige Economics

PRESTIGE ECONOMICS

Current State of the U.S. Labor Market

After having examined the current state of (and the near-term expectations for) the U.S. labor market, it should be easy to see how the current state of work has changed dramatically in recent decades. Agricultural jobs are almost extinct, manufacturing jobs have been in decline since 1979, and healthcare is on the rise.

Understanding that productivity is a key driver of automation, robotics, and computerization is critical. Simply put: employers want to get more bang for their buck, and automation presents that opportunity. I think we can all agree that there will be big changes in the future of work. What that future looks like, however, and how the labor market will change, is at the heart of the debate between Robocalypse and Robotopia.

In the next two chapters, I lay out the downside risks of a Robocalypse, as well as the upside potential for a Robotopia. Automation will be critical for our professional lives, and while the future could go either way, I think the end result is somewhere in between. But, it will depend quite a bit on how we lever the opportunities we have — a subject I cover deeply in Chapter 8 and Chapter 9.

CHAPTER 4

ROBOCALYPSE: DOWNSIDE FOR THE FUTURE OF WORK

In the debate of Robocalypse versus Robotopia, the Robocalypse camp likes to argue that *"This time is different."* Prophets of Robocalypse argue that there are four key fundamental differences *this time,* that will usher in a harrowing end to our world:

People will be unable to keep up with labor market changes.

All jobs will disappear.

People will have no purpose.

Computers will run amok.

But, this time is *never* different. In the automation age, some jobs will cease to exist in the way that most typist, copy boy, and toll booth attendant jobs have already vanished. And don't forget the blacksmiths, millers, and weavers from Chapter 2.

Regardless of technological advancements, people will still have — and need— things to do.

Robocalypse Claim: People Will be Unable to Keep Up

Robocalypse prophets argue that changes in the nature of work during the automation age will be unlike any others in history. While I agree that these changes will come fast and furious — at a pace we have never seen before, I believe that the magnitude of change is likely to be smaller.

As we saw in Chapter 2, the industrial revolution upended economic structures that had been in place for centuries, if not millennia. But a number of factors are likely to remain similar in the automation age: the nature of most work will still be service, most jobs will still require skills or education, and most working conditions will still be generally professional, as opposed to agricultural or industrial. Automation is likely to exacerbate the premium placed on intellectual work and education, while the trend to remote working environments will accelerate. These are much smaller changes than those seen in the transitions of the industrial revolution.

It will be a challenge to keep up in the automation age, but we have no choice. A big advantage is that we know that the economy is dynamic. And we know automation and robots are coming. We also know the value of, and have access to, more education opportunities than ever before. As such, we are also better prepared for secular changes in the labor market than ever before. Of course, we could be even better prepared. But, low-skill, low-income, and low-education jobs are the most at risk of Robocalypse. The robots are coming for those jobs.

Robocalypse Claim: All Jobs Will Disappear

Robocalypse prophets argue that all jobs will be automated out of existence. While some jobs will vanish, others are less vulnerable.

Automation will affect jobs, but the labor market is likely to experience a bifurcated set of dynamics, with education and skills as critical dividers. As you can see in Figure 4-1, Some sectors, like manufacturing and transportation, have high technical potential for automation. But other sectors like education, management, professionals, information, and healthcare have much lower automation potential. In other words, Robocalypse is a much lower risk for educated professionals.

Figure 4-1: Sector Potential for Automation[1]

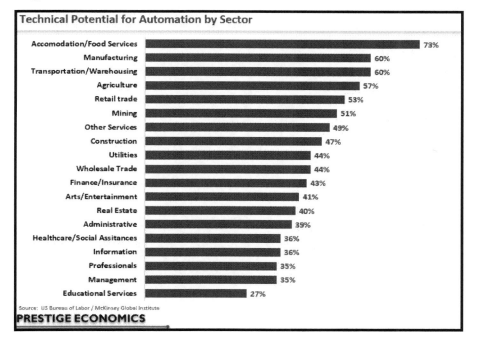

Robocalypse Reality: Low-Skill Jobs Will Disappear

There will be a Robocalypse for low-skill and low-income jobs — especially those with repetitive manual tasks. According to a study of automation by the McKinsey Global Institute, the most manual and lowest-skill jobs are at risk of the greatest automation potential.[2] This is reflected in Figure 4-2. While this data reflect bifurcated risks, it does not reflect the potential for an all-out Robocalypse.

On a side note, I am happy to see statisticians are pretty low on the list for automation potential. I would imagine that futurists would be even lower on the list, given the longer time horizon of analytical reference, in which most futurists operate.

Figure 4-2: Low-Skill Jobs Have High Automation Potential[3]

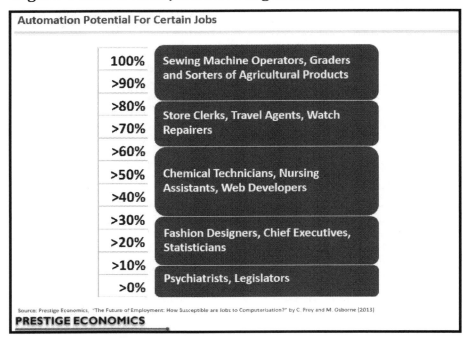

Automation Potential For Certain Jobs

100%	Sewing Machine Operators, Graders and Sorters of Agricultural Products
>90%	
>80%	Store Clerks, Travel Agents, Watch Repairers
>70%	
>60%	
>50%	Chemical Technicians, Nursing Assistants, Web Developers
>40%	
>30%	Fashion Designers, Chief Executives, Statisticians
>20%	
>10%	
>0%	Psychiatrists, Legislators

Source: Prestige Economics, "The Future of Employment: How Susceptible are Jobs to Computerisation?" by C. Frey and M. Osborne (2013)

PRESTIGE ECONOMICS

Robocalypse Reality: Low-Income Jobs Will Disappear

In addition to a Robocalypse of low-skill jobs, there is a risk of a Robocalypse for low-income jobs. In Figure 4-3, you can see how 83 percent of jobs that pay less than $20 per hour have a high probability of automation, while jobs that pay more than $40 per hour only have a 4 percent chance of automation.[4]

This economic division underscores the need for policies to help smoothly transition workers who lose their jobs to automation. Access to skill-building opportunities will be critical. Otherwise, there is a risk that economic distress would spill over into the political arena. And a lack of opportunity to build skills could sow the seeds of universal basic income that you will find in Chapter 7.

Figure 4-3: Low-Income Jobs at High Risk of Automation[5]

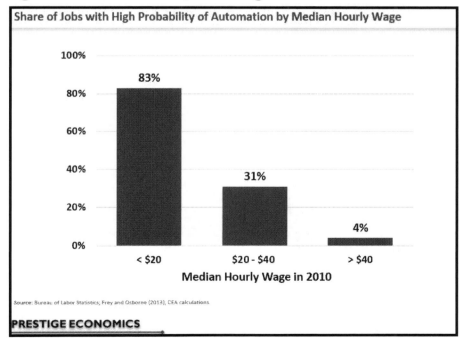

Share of Jobs with High Probability of Automation by Median Hourly Wage

Source: Bureau of Labor Statistics; Frey and Osborne (2013), CEA calculations

PRESTIGE ECONOMICS

Robocalypse Reality: Low-Education Jobs Will Disappear

Jobs that require only low levels of education are also at risk of Robocalypse, along with low-income jobs. A report issued by the Office of the President in December 2016 titled, "Artificial Intelligence, Automation, and the Economy," included data about low-income and low-income jobs seen in Figures 4-3 and 4-4.[6]

According to the report, 44 percent of jobs that require less than a high school diploma are "highly automatable," while zero jobs that require graduate degrees are "highly automatable." Zero. Plus, only one percent of jobs that require a Bachelor's degree are viewed as highly automatable. This graph shows the value of education in protecting yourself from being a victim of Robocalypse.

Figure 4-4: Lower Education Jobs at High Risk of Automation[7]

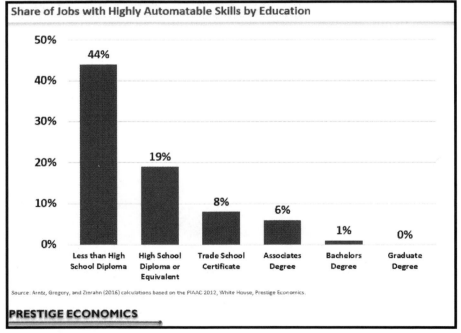

Source: Arntz, Gregory, and Zierahn (2016) calculations based on the PIAAC 2012, White House, Prestige Economics.

PRESTIGE ECONOMICS

Global Robocalypse Risks[8]

So how many jobs are at risk due to automation? It depends very much on who you ask. There have been a number of studies conducted on the impact of automation. One of the leading studies from Frey and Osborne in 2013 showed that about 47 percent of U.S. jobs are at high risk of automation. Frey and Osborne also argued that risks of automation were even more significant abroad, as follows:

OECD automation potential around 57 percent.
Chinese automation potential around 77 percent.
Indian automation potential around 69 percent.

As if these predictions were not dismal enough, McKinsey sees an even more apocalyptic vision of Robocalypse, with half of all global activities potentially automatable.[9]

Regional Robocalypse Risks

In my book, *Recession-Proof*, I noted that recessions can be isolated to certain regions. So, too, it seems that certain regions are more exposed to automation risks than others. This is particularly true in areas where there is low-cost manufacturing.

For decades, many economists have predicted that all low-cost manufacturing would eventually end up in Africa. But, based on the potential for low-skill jobs to be automated, robots could turn out to be the lowest cost option, rather than the geographic labor cost arbitrage available from a relocation of manufacturing facilities to Africa.

Robocalypse Risks in U.S. Cities

While a Robocalypse is unlikely for the entire U.S. or global economies, certain cities are more exposed than others.

Given the factors that put workers at risk of Robocalypse, and the upside potential for tech and innovation hubs, it stands to reason that cities with highly-educated, highly-skilled, and high-income workforces are naturally at the lowest risk of a regional Robocalypse. In Figure 4-5, you can see a list of the most and least at-risk U.S. cities.

Figure 4-5: U.S. Cities Exposed[10]

Automation Risk by City		
Most At Risk		**Least At Risk**
Fresno	53.8% — 38.4%	Washington D.C.
Las Vegas	49.1% — 38.4%	Boston
Greensboro	48.5% — 39.7%	Raleigh
Reading	48.4% — 40.4%	Baltimore
Grand Rapids	47.9% — 40.7%	New York
Oklahoma City	47.1% — 41.1%	Bridgeport
Harrisburg	47.1% — 41.2%	Toms River
Los Angeles	47.0% — 41.4%	Minneapolis
Dayton	46.0% — 41.4%	Richmond
Sacramento	45.9% — 41.5%	Denver
Houston	45.8% — 41.7%	San Francisco

Source: World Economic Forum, Prestige Economics

PRESTIGE ECONOMICS

The bifurcated composition of the most at risk and least at risk cities in Figure 4-5 seems to hold true to the notion that education, income, and skill are the defining factors of success or failure. Enrico Moretti, a professor of economics at the University of California at Berkley, notes in his book *The New Geography of Jobs* that economic development effects are "profoundly different in different cities and regions of the country" in such a way that favors "the residents of some cities and hurt[s] the residents of others...[as part of a] redistribution of jobs, population and wealth" to tech and innovation hubs, which is "likely to accelerate in the decades to come."[11] In other words, tech hubs are likely to be more insulated from the risk of a potential Robocalypse. And those cities with heavy tech and innovation sectors could even continue to grow.

Conversely, cities with low-skill, low-education, and low-income workforces are, in aggregate, putting their cities at a greater risk of Robocalypse. This is the likely driver behind the different risks of automation for the U.S. cities in Figure 4-5.[12]

The professional risks and challenges that could face a large number of workers are not new. In recent years, globalization has weighed on regions with low-skilled workers. And long before that, the risk of technological unemployment had been a risk and concern at various times since John Maynard Keynes coined the term in 1930. Put simply, technological unemployment is unemployment that occurs independently of the business cycle. It is the explicit result of technological advances that do not benefit the entire population — a risk we now face with automation.

Technological Unemployment

A Robocalypse in certain industries would be more than just a period of job loss, but a complete destruction of entire industries due to changes in technology. These changes could leave large numbers of workers unemployed because they are *unemployable*, and their skills are no longer needed. The economist John Maynard Keynes is credited with the concept of technological unemployment, writing in 1930:

> We are being afflicted with a new disease of which some readers may not yet have heard the name, but of which they will hear a great deal in the years to come — namely, technological unemployment. This means unemployment due to our discovery of means of economising the use of labour outrunning the pace at which we can find new uses for labour. But this is only a temporary phase of maladjustment. All this means in the long run that mankind is solving its economic problem. I would predict that the standard of life in progressive countries one hundred years hence will be between four and eight times as high as it is to-day. There would be nothing surprising in this even in the light of our present knowledge. It would not be foolish to contemplate the possibility of a far greater progress still."[13]

Keynes described challenges that were similar to the ones presented today by the prospects of automation and robotics. In his writing, you can read his concerns about disruption, but also his hope for higher productivity, growth, income, and skills.

One such area of great concern today is transportation.

Transpocalypse

Perhaps the field most at risk of a Robocalypse and massive job losses is transportation. According to BLS estimates shown in Figure 4-6, between 2.2 and 3.1 million transportation jobs are threatened by automation.[14] Anyone getting into transportation as a job needs to know that these are milk carton careers; they have an expiration date — and it's sometime soon.

Even if jobs in transportation vanish — and they will — there are still upside factors. At the most basic level, automated self-driving vehicles appear to be safer, since they do not drink, text, sleep, or get distracted at the wheel. One estimate shows self-driving vehicles could save 33,000 American lives per year.[15]

Figure 4-6: Transportation Jobs at Risk[16]

Transportation Jobs Threatened by Automation

Occupation	# Total Jobs (BLS, May 2015)	Range of Replacement Weights	Range of # Jobs Threatened
Bus Drivers, Transit and Intercity	168,620	0.60 – 1.0	101,170 – 168,620
Light Truck or Delivery Services Drivers	826,510	0.20 – 0.60	165,300 – 495,910
Heavy and Tractor-Trailer Truck Drivers	1,678,280	0.80 – 1.0	1,342,620 – 1,678,280
Bus Drivers, School or Special Client	505,560	0.30 – 0.40	151,670 – 202,220
Taxi Drivers and Chauffeurs	180,960	0.60 – 1.0	108,580 – 180,960
Self-employed drivers	364,000	0.90 – 1.0	328,000 – 364,000
TOTAL JOBS	3,723,930		2,196,940 – 3,089,990

Source: BLS, Prestige Economics

PRESTIGE ECONOMICS

We don't bemoan the fact that when we eat bread, the flour wasn't ground by a miller in a local village mill between two stones powered by wind or water. And someday, we might not bemoan the fact that trucks drive themselves, and "truck driver" is no longer a common profession.

I will discuss some of the economic upside potential presented by automation of vehicles in Chapter 5. For now, let's examine a Robocalypse risk beyond transportation that affects workers with high skills, high levels of education, and high levels of income.

Robocalypse Beyond Transportation

Aside from the Transpocalypse, some futurists, like Jerry Kaplan, have noted that "advances in information technology are already gutting industries and jobs at a furious clip, far faster than the labor markets can possibly adapt, and there's much worse to come."[17] Kaplan also notes that "the holy grail of Silicon Valley entrepreneurs is the disruption of entire industries – because that's where the big money is to be made."[18]

But the biggest money to be made from automation and disruption is nowhere near transportation. The biggest money to be made will be from disrupting money itself. In traditional financial services, and on Wall Street, robots have arrived. There is even a term for this type of disruption: FinTech.

Yes, the robots are coming for low-skill, low-income, and low-education jobs. But, they are coming for other jobs, too. I learned not too long ago that they are coming for mine.

You Might Not Hear The Robots Coming

The first time I heard the word FinTech, I was at the Atlanta Federal Reserve Bank's Financial Markets Conference on Amelia Island. At this annual meeting, which I have attended for seven years, about 100 of the world's top economists are invited to join regional Fed bank presidents, government regulators, academics, and often the Chairman of the Federal Reserve, to discuss the hottest economic, monetary policy, and fiscal policy issues of the day.

Against a backdrop of this prestigious conference, a Fed reporter I have known for years and I skipped out of some sessions to enjoy the beautiful early May Florida weather. My friend was with another reporter whose specialty was FinTech. At the time, I had not yet heard of FinTech. So, I asked innocently "What's that?" The reporter told me FinTech was "like Bitcoin and stuff like that." I knew Bitcoin was an electronic currency, so that was that. I didn't think too much of this conversation until several months later, when I tried to hire a salesperson for Prestige Economics. I had difficulty finding candidates. Highly qualified people were exiting the space in droves. And I didn't know why.

Finally, one senior salesperson told me that everyone was getting out of financial market research, because of FinTech. Essentially, the robots were disrupting the research business. After being told that FinTech was disrupting the my own business, I decided to learn as much as possible about it by taking a FinTech course at MIT. In short, the robots have been coming for me, and I didn't even know it.

FinTech: Robocalypse Comes to Finance

FinTech is a buzzword for financial technology, which represents a host of businesses that are designed to disrupt (and eat the lunch of) traditional financial institutions. FinTech companies generally reduce costs, reduce complexity, or increase ease of use for transactions that had previously been the domain of banks.

FinTech is affecting financial services and awareness is spreading. The poster in Figure 4-7 was hanging in the Jacksonville airport in 2016 — the same airport I flew into for the Fed conference where I first heard the word FinTech. But, Jacksonville is not a FinTech hub. As such, the presence of this poster implies that awareness about the automation of work, FinTech, and Roboadvising is widespread.

Figure 4-7: Jobs For Robots in Jacksonville, Florida[19]

Roboadvising: Robocalypse for Active Asset Management

Asset management has long been dominated by computers, statistical analysis, and programming. In Figure 4-9, you can see FinTech is disrupting asset management — often with passive trading strategies known as Roboadvising, due to their automated nature. This is the subject of Figure 4-8.

In the movie *Wall Street*, Gordon Gekko asks Bud Fox, "Ever wonder why fund managers can't beat the S&P 500?" Well, with the advent of Exchange Traded Funds (ETFs), fund managers and retail investors can just buy the S&P, which is what they have done. And, a number of ETFs are very liquidly traded.

Figure 4-8: Impact of FinTech on Financial Advice[20]

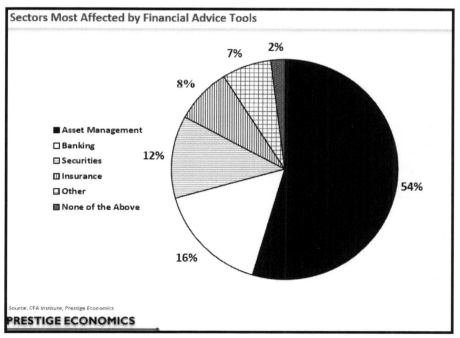

Sectors Most Affected by Financial Advice Tools

- Asset Management
- Banking
- Securities
- Insurance
- Other
- None of the Above

7% 2%
8%
12%
54%
16%

Source: CFA Institute, Prestige Economics

PRESTIGE ECONOMICS

Another big positive, is that passive asset management techniques and Roboadvising are often easier and cheaper to administer than active asset management. These strategies can be implemented at significantly lower costs than active asset management strategies, because they no longer require human asset managers. There is an economy of scale, when computer programs do all the strategy work, analysis, and planning, as well as all of the buying and selling of securities.

Passive asset management has also been adopted by a field that has historically embraced technology, with many firms using black box, algorithmic, and technical trading strategies for some time. Expensive items (like market research) are also no longer parts of the budget, since decisions are made by computers. After all, trading computer programs do not read words. But they like lines — especially lines above which (or below which) the price of a traded security has consistently stayed for a long time.

In Figure 4-9, you can see gold prices with some critical trading technicals. The image shows how gold prices fell hard and fast after closing just below an upward-sloping technical support (upward-sloping blue diagonal line) that had been in place (and supported) from December 2015 until the end of September 2016. Prices were above that line for a relatively long time. And it was a line the computers were watching. It was also a level that I highlighted in our research frequently over the course of many months. As you can see in the chart, before a big selloff, there was a price drop below the blue upward-sloping diagonal. Essentially, you saw the technical traders in the market selling gold hard and fast, once certain critical trading lines were broken.

Technical trading has become more important, so analysts have been trying to add value by knowing what lines and supports matter most for the computers in different markets.

This is why there has been a significant increase in the number of financial professionals pursuing the Chartered Market Technician® designation over the past year. The CMT® — a designation I completed last year — focuses exclusively on these kinds of technical trading dynamics. Essentially, you are looking for the computers in the market. I expect these kinds of trading dynamics will continue to become increasingly important, as passive asset management and Roboadvising continue to grow.

Figure 4-9: Gold Prices Show Importance of Technicals[21]

Robocalypse Claim: People Will Have no Purpose

Robocalypse prophets also argue that people will have no purpose in the future. But, it is my expectation that people will have jobs for a long time to come. Plus, just because automation can occur, does not mean that it will. Technology can take a long time to spread. After all, think about the fact that 783 million people do not have access to clean water,[22] 2.5 billion people do not have access to adequate sanitation,[23] and 1.2 billion people do not have access to electricity.[24] These technologies are relatively old, and the fact that a large chunk of the world is still underdeveloped indicates to me that people will have jobs for a long time to come. In Chapter 5, I will share some information on upside opportunities for the labor force, as automation increases.

Robocalypse Claim: Computers Will Run Amok

The final claim of Robocalypse prophets, is that computers will run amok, destroying the world and all the people in it. This is the well from which every Robocalypse film springs. There is also a real reason to be concerned.

We need look no further than the miserable failure of Microsoft's attempt to expose its artificial intelligence (AI) pet project, Tay, to the world via Twitter. In less than a day, Tay had learned some very bad things like racism, rabid anti-Semitism, and other forms of unfiltered hate.[25] Naturally, the project was shut down quickly. And I also expect it will be some time, before anyone lets its AI project out in public again. The risk computers will run amok, is a real problem that highlights the increasingly important need for project, process, and program management skills. I discuss this topic extensively in Chapter 9.

Robocalypse-Watch: New York Almost at Peak Automation

Before we leave the topic of Robocalypse behind, I want to share a personal story. In the fall of 2016, I took a media and client trip to New York City. Perhaps because I was working on this book, I noticed the big role automation and robotics already play there.

Using a kiosk, I checked into my room at the Yotel (yes, you read that correctly). Then, I bought food across the street at a CVS using an automated checkout machine. After a night and day of meetings, I checked out of my hotel and left my luggage with a robot, called the Yobot, which you can see in Figure 4-10. Then, after retrieving my luggage late in the day from said robot, I went to the airport, where I ordered sushi from a tablet without speaking to a soul. Aside from the clients and journalists I met with, my trip was highly automated. Obviously, labor costs are very high in New York, so automation might be logical there.

Figure 4-10: Bellman of the Future, "Yobot" in NYC[26]

Given the abundance of automation on my trip, I wondered if this could be a sign of the coming Robocalypse. But I suppose it is a bit much to label a robot bellman as one of the four horsemen of the Robocalypse?

And yet, I still wonder what will happen when this level of automation and robotics comes to Topeka, Bakersfield, Tampa, and Austin? I suspect that it might just be a while before the ROI is there.

Something that could hasten automation would be tax policies that incentivize employers to de-people their workforces. As you will see in Chapter 6, there are growing incentives for employers to automate less-skilled jobs. Risks of higher payroll taxes to fund unfunded entitlements, combined with rising employee health care costs, and potentially accompanied by higher minimum wage laws, could usher in an unnecessary Robocalypse by providing the kinds of tax incentives that decimate jobs.

CHAPTER 5

ROBOTOPIA: UPSIDE FOR THE FUTURE OF WORK

Robotopia in its purest form would be a world where robots do all the work, and people have unlimited leisure. To harken back to one of the original visions of utopia, I would like to note that Thomas More's sixteenth-century novel *Utopia* was "a description of an ideal state in which social evils such as poverty and despair have been eliminated."[1] Indeed, many speak of a coming Robotopia in the same way.

For some, this world of complete and total leisure also comes with free money, often benignly referred to as universal basic income (UBI). In Chapter 7, I will share why a full Robotopia, in which no one works and everyone receives UBI, is likely to prove unfulfilling and problematic for society. For now, let's focus on the realistically achievable upside potential of automation.

"Utopia" is Greek for nowhere. And automation and robots are likely to usher in a perfect world exactly nowhere; there will be no messianic age of robots. But there will be plenty of benefits and advantages!

Robots Bring Freedom

In the automation age, people will have more **free time**, they will have more **freedom of movement**, and they will have more **freedom of choice** when it comes to goods and services. Plus, people will likely pay less for things in the future that cost a fortune today. Let's start by looking at free time.

Work Free Time

According to research by the McKinsey Global Institute, 30 percent of the activities performed by 62 percent of occupations could be automated.[2] You can see this in Figure 5-1. One interesting note is that only 1 percent of jobs has been identified as fully automatable.

As such, increased automation in the workplace does not mean that it will force people out of work. Secretaries were a leading occupation in 21 states in 1978, and even I took typing courses in the late 1980s. Today, we are all typists. More automation could further free up our time for more interesting, enriching, and intellectually challenging tasks.

The top three kinds of activities that McKinsey identifies as "activities with highest automation potential" are "predictable physical activities" at 81 percent, "processing data" at 69 percent, and "collecting data" at 64 percent.[3] Analyzing data is more critical than collecting it, and physical activities in warehouses and factories entered the automation age decades ago. But, more of these physical tasks could be automated.

Figure 5-1: McKinsey Analysis of Automation Potential[4]

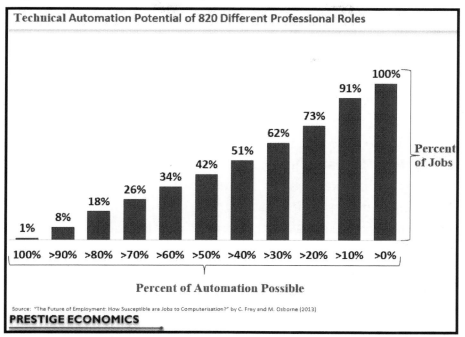

Technical Automation Potential of 820 Different Professional Roles

Percent of Jobs:
- 100%: 1%
- >90%: 8%
- >80%: 18%
- >70%: 26%
- >60%: 34%
- >50%: 42%
- >40%: 51%
- >30%: 62%
- >20%: 73%
- >10%: 91%
- >0%: 100%

Percent of Automation Possible

Source: "The Future of Employment: How Susceptible are Jobs to Computerisation?" by C. Frey and M. Osborne (2013)

PRESTIGE ECONOMICS

Personal Free Time

I saw a meme recently titled, "The Neverending Story." It was a split image of two pictures. The top picture from the eponymous film including the words "as a child" above a picture of the dog-like Falkor the Luck Dragon. The bottom picture included the words "as an adult" above a picture of a big pile of dirty laundry.[5]

It's funny, because it's true. Of course, it would be significantly less funny to people living before washing machines. Having lived in Europe, it is also less funny without dryers. But clothes can be air dried. Still, can you image lugging bucket after bucket of clothes down to a river to wash them?

This is what people did for most of time — and what they still do in some places. But, I do not see anyone bemoaning the automation of washing clothes. In fact, there are currently prototypes of washing machines that will wash, dry, and fold your laundry. Can you imagine how much free time you would have if your laundry was washed, dried, and folded by one machine? Sign me up!

And this is probably just the beginning. As with the future of work, robot applications in our day-to-day lives will be focused on doing the most unpleasant or difficult tasks. Experts in the robotics world joke that people cannot wait for robots that can be programmed to clean bathrooms. It's at the top of the list. It's above changing light bulbs — and it might even be above doing the laundry.

Maximizing Benefits: Cloud Computing for Robots

James Kuffner, the Chief Technology Officer of the Toyota Research Institute, while speaking at the Robobusiness conference in San Jose, California in September 2016, noted that one of the most critical developments for robots of the next 50 years would be cloud robotics.[6] In the same way that apps, self-driving cars, and other technology can learn and report back to a centralized cloud to improve performance of all connected devices, the same is likely to happen to robots.

With the use of cloud computing, robots don't need to be individually taught. A program can be downloaded, lessons can be learned on an individual machine, and results can be uploaded and shared with the entire cloud network of other robots.

As the futurist Kurzweil has noted, "Machines can pool their resources in ways that humans cannot."[7] Their ability to learn from each other through a central reservoir of experience in the cloud should accelerate their technological advancement.

Free Your Time at Hardware Stores

Some retail does not work well as in-hand retail. Hardware stores are a great example, because of the often cumbersome nature of the goods, and the relatively low cost of very heavy items. Plus, if you're like me, I always find myself being told that items are in two different rows at opposite ends of the store, Need a hammer? Row 3 or 58. Smoke detectors? Row 14 or 31.

Perhaps this is why the hardware chain Lowe's developed a customer-facing robot to work in its stores that is in Figure 5-2. This robot can show shoppers where goods are. However, it actually has a much more valuable function: it can perform labor-intensive inventory counts while guiding customers around the store.

Figure 5-2: LoweBot[9]

In this manner, the robot can replace a greeter, as well as accountants doing audits — replacing both low and high skill jobs. According to the World Economic Forum, 75% of respondents expect 30% of corporate audits performed by artificial intelligence by 2025.[8]

Amazon Go

Another example of technology that has the potential to free your time is Amazon Go. The concept store in Seattle (Figure 5-3) allows shoppers to buy groceries without ever having to go through a checkout line. Technology in the store recognizes when you take something (or put it back), and you are charged automatically for goods in your possession, when you walk out of the store.

You might enjoy grocery shopping because you — like me, like everyone — are a commodity fetishist at heart. You want to go buy stuff, and you might prefer to buy food in person because it's produce; you want to see and touch it, before you buy it. Even as more retail goes online, restaurants, food service, and grocery stores are likely to remain critical parts of the physical retail economy.

Figure 5-3: Amazon Go[10]

However, you might be wasting time in line at the grocery store. This is why fully automated shopping with instantaneous checkout presents upside opportunities to liberate your time. Plus, grocery store kiosks have largely been a failure.

Upside for Retailers

There are also significant potential benefits to retailers from this kind of store, because it could reduce theft and waste. Theft risk would fall. because it would be more difficult for shoppers to leave the store without paying for items. Meanwhile. waste could fall, since inventories could be monitored in real time, and restocking could be done with just-in-time orders.

In retail, theft and waste — known as shrinkage — are major costs to grocery stores. In fact, a 2015 University of Florida study showed that grocery stores and supermarkets reported "the highest average shrinkage calculated at retail."[11] Supermarkets reported shrinkage at an average of 3.23 percent, compared to 1.17 percent at sporting goods and recreational retailers.[12] Reducing shrinkage would be a very big deal.

In sum, Amazon Go technology could reduce transaction friction, save customer time, and even help with owner loss prevention — reducing costs and improving profits.

I just hope the tech is as good as it could be valuable.

Free Your Time in Self-Driving Cars

Self-driving cars present tremendous opportunities to free your time during rush hour (or even during off-peak times). You could be productively working or just relaxing, instead of focusing on driving — something a robot will happily do for you. Although this threatens to disrupt transportation services and livery companies, those firms have already been significantly disrupted by ride-sharing apps.

Free Your Movement in Self-Driving Cars

In addition to freeing your time, self-driving cars also present the opportunity to free your movement. People too young to drive, too old to drive, or who are incapacitated, injured, or disabled, could safely find on-demand transportation 24/7. Self-driving car technology and products have been in development for years, and Waymo (Figures 5-4 and 5-5) has logged millions of miles with its technology. Tesla has done the same.

Figure 5-4: Waymo Vehicle with Self-Driving Technology[13]

Based on my own experience, self-driving car technology appears to be pretty ready for rollout. In fact, I hope my next car will be self-driving — and I own a 2008 car.

Several companies are working on self-driving cars, which many believe could be provided in fleet form on a software as a service (SaaS) model. As noted in *The Economist*:

> The car industry....increasingly sees its future in the provision of "mobility services" rather than as a seller of boxes with wheels at the corners. Running their own fleets of cars with which to offer autonomous or shared rides looks to many like the wave of the future—and possibly a very profitable one.[14]

There is one big challenge to the SaaS model for self-driving cars. As my wife is quick to note: *People are gross.*

You've heard stories of what people have done in taxis or ride-shares with a human driver in close proximity. What do you think will happen when no one is there? What will people leave behind? Trash? Half-eaten food? Vomit? Dirty diapers? What if a child decides to poop in one on the way to soccer practice?

I mean, would you want to ride in a self-driving fleet car at night on "Thirsty Thursday" in a college town?

Creating Jobs For Humans

Self-driving cars could be automatically dispatched and there may be ways to automate the fueling/charging of fleets of these vehicles. However, given the aforementioned practical concerns, monitoring people in the cars, cleaning the cars, and taking them offline (if the grossness is extreme) are likely to be jobs for people.

On the upside, this would create jobs. And one person could remotely monitor a number of different automated rideshare vehicles at the same time. But, the point is: riders will need to be monitored, and people will need to do the monitoring.

This means that, even if fleet SaaS options for self-driving vehicles were available, I would greatly prefer to just buy my own. After all, I'd like to trick it out with a desk I could work at, a really nice chair, a tiny cactus, a small bookshelf, and a dog bed for our Chigi, Honey. Wouldn't you like to customize your new mobile office/living room?

Figure 5-5: No Hands: Waymo Without a Steering Wheel[15]

Expectations for Driverless Cars

Based on September 2015 survey data from the World Economic Forum, 79 percent of respondents expect 10 percent of cars will be driverless by 2025.[16] This is more aggressive than EIA forecasts of future electric vehicles, which are only expected to be between 1 and 6 percent of new U.S. vehicles through 2040.[17]

Freedom of Choice

In addition to freeing your time and your movement, there are a number of technologies that will also increase your freedom of choice with regard to consumption. Some of these will also inherently free up your time. In Figure 5-6, you can see one of the clearest manifestations of increased choice: e-commerce. In Q4 2016, it was 8.3 percent of all retail sales. And it is going to rise further.

Figure 5-6: E-commerce Retail as a Percent of Total Sales[18]

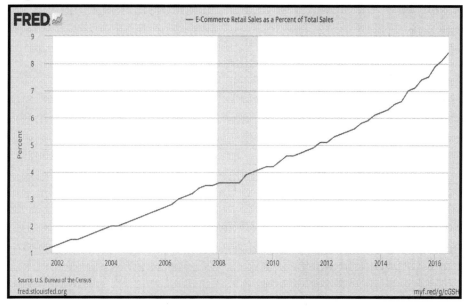

Material Handling to the Rescue

In order to meet the demand of an accelerated pace of e-commerce, we need to go beyond what humans can do. Historically, the distribution supply chain involved shipping goods from warehouses to retail stores by pallets or batches. Individuals would then go to retail stores to acquire their goods. This is still how the vast majority of retail happens, with 91.7 percent of all U.S. retail sales at brick and mortar in Q4 2016.

With e-commerce, however, everyone's smart phone is effectively a store front, and goods can be delivered to you. Your couch, your kitchen, or wherever your laptop and your smart phone are: that's your retail. But, it's more than that. It's more than at-home retail, it's in-hand retail.

For example, I've had things delivered to hotels when I travel. On extended trips, when I knew I would run out of clean clothes, I've ordered things online ahead for myself: t-shirts, socks, dress shirts, underwear, ties, and even cowboy boots. I know a lot of other people who are frequent travellers who do not yet do this. But, often it is easier and cheaper than bringing a suitcase. These kinds of realities will continue to drive e-commerce levels higher and higher.

In-hand retail is going to be a thing that continues to drive the need for automation and robotics in a very positive way. It is also something that will continue to stress the U.S. supply chain and the abilities of material handling equipment and technology to keep up with demand that is going to rise much further.

Single-Piece Flow Demands Robotics and Automation

Material handling is one of the areas where we see tremendous upside potential to enhance life and improve consumer access to goods, by meeting the rising demands of in-home and in-hand retail. Kevin Vliet, a supply chain executive at the Target Corporation with 25-years of experience including previous stints at Tesla, Amazon, and Ford, pointed out to me in a recent conversation that the U.S. economy is "not set up for single-piece flow of goods through supply chains."[19] In other words, if we all want our individual, single-piece orders now, we need to realize that there are too many things for humans to pull and pack in a warehouse. Robots and automation are the only solutions to solve the rising tide of consumer demand for e-commerce goods that keeps goods flowing — and affordable.

Last Mile Issues

Robots don't necessarily need to work in a retail store but when the retail store becomes your hand, you need robots to make that last mile work. For this reason, problems in transportation and retail have become last mile delivery problems. This is still where there are opportunities for greater efficiency — sending goods from warehouses to people's homes. And this is where there is the potential for an automated last mile delivery optimization system that could account for how items are placed on a truck and how they are dropped off, so that the process conserves both fuel and time.

Consumers Love Supply Chains

Automation and robotics are going to accelerate at a more rapid pace. And these have the potential to keep costs down, helping customers get goods faster and cheaper. They help people get the in-hand retail they want — and will want, with increasing volume demands. As Thomas Friedman noted in his book, *The World is Flat,* "as consumers, we love supply chains, because they deliver us all sorts of goods...at lower and lower prices and tailored more and more precisely to just what we want."[20]

This is a notion I have heard from my clients in the material handling and supply chain worlds. The only way to give 319 million people exactly what they want as individuals at any time, day or night, is to leverage a supply chain and distribution network that can make the magic happen. Friedman notes that "a smart and fast global supply chain is becoming one of the most important ways for a company to distinguish itself from its competitors."[21] But, the truth is: *The best supply chain is one you don't see, hear about, or even think about.* It just works.

The Singulatarian Ray Kurzweil has also acknowledged the importance of logistics, noting that "Computer-integrated manufacturing (CIM) increasingly employs AI techniques to optimize the use of resources, streamline logistics, and reduce inventories through just-in-time purchasing of parts and supplies."[22] At the retail level, this is something LoweBot (Figure 5-2) does by performing real-time inventory audits, and placing just-in-time orders when inventories fall too low. Amazon Go also seems likely to do real-time monitoring of inventories and replenish with just-in-time orders. Even kiosks may play a role.

Kioskification is Good

The biggest professional secret I present in my book, *Recession-Proof,* is to fly first class to maximize professional opportunities. I have seen a few recent articles online, in which the authors belligerently ask if the people sitting in first class are millionaires and CEOs. To those guys, I say: Yes. They are.

In the fall of 2016, as I was working on *Jobs for Robots*, I was lucky enough to sit next to Tony Muscarello, the Executive Vice President of Sales for Cardtronics — the world's largest non-bank ATM operator.[23] Over the course of a three-hour flight, I was able to interview this expert in the field of automation, whose company manages over 200,000 ATMs. It was just good luck. And it would not have happened, if I had flown coach.

Tony shared a few critical thoughts that have shaped my thinking about kiosks and the prospects for future kioskification. The first — and most important — thing he told me was that "the self-service revolution is real." He stated directly that ATMs and kiosks have emerged to meet consumer demand. And as Americans become more acculturated to kiosks, the kioskification of America will accelerate. And yet, since these ATMs and kiosks feed an unmet new demand, they are unlikely to take jobs away from people. This is because, according to Tony, the success of kiosks is predicated on simplicity of use. He noted that, "While advanced functionality is sexy, it's often tough to make money."

One ATM that has a simple functionality that highlights the upside risks of kiosks is a cupcake ATM in Austin.

Figure 5-7: Cupcakes 24/7 — Thanks Robots![24]

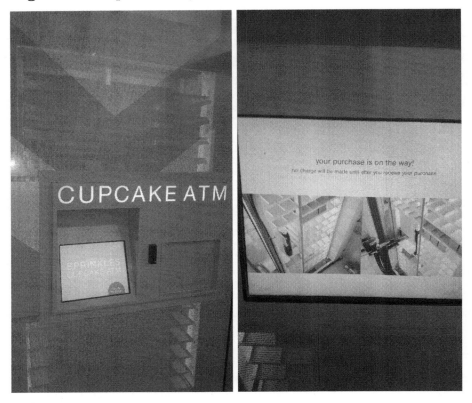

ATMs of the Future

Even if we end up in a future cashless society, there will still a need for ATMs...that dispense cupcakes! In Figure 5-7, you can see the cupcake ATM that was installed in Austin, Texas in February 2017 by a company called Sprinkles. On the right, you can see a robot arm grabbing and dispensing the cupcake I ordered.[25] This kind of self-service technology is a rare oddity now, but it is likely to become increasingly ubiquitous. And this kind of 24/7 self-service robot could be positive for human job creation during normal, waking business hours.

Most economists would tell you that specialization is good for businesses and the economy. This is also likely to prove true with our cupcake ATM example. After all, the highest value of someone who handmakes cupcakes is not in selling cupcakes; it's in making cupcakes. And this cupcake ATM only sells cupcakes. This helps create more meaningful work for humans involved in the business. After all, cupcake makers would presumably enjoy making cupcakes more than they enjoy selling them.

This system works, because the kiosk is not performing a complicated function. It requires a robotic arm and some material handling technology, but its functionality is relatively limited. It just sells cupcakes. And it sells cupcakes that might otherwise not be sold, since the ATM can sell cupcakes even when the store is closed and even when the store has a line that might otherwise deter customers.

Because of increased sales through an automated delivery system, there would likely be an increased need for more human work to handmake additional cupcakes during normal business hours, because of sales that occur when the store is closed. In this way, a self-service food kiosk creates not only more meaningful work, but it also creates a need for additional human work.

Cupcake ATMs present a vision of kioskification that should be positive for job gains, as the self-service revolution continues. since they fill demand for goods that previously could not be met.

Cupcakes with Other Non-Tech Jobs on Top

In addition to creating better access to cupcakes, if a tech company is responsible for installing that cupcake ATM, that would be good for the local economy. As more tasks are automated, there is also likely to be a greater need for high-tech workers. And high-tech jobs also bring more work for others. According to Moretti, "Attracting a scientist or a software engineer to a city triggers a *multiplier effect*, increasing employment and salaries for those who provide local services."[26] As such, that one job creates other jobs.

Moretti also notes that the manufacturing multiplier is 1.6: for each job created or lost, add or detract 1.6 additional jobs, respectively. This is why areas that lose manufacturing jobs tend to be hit hard economically. For each manufacturing job they lose, they are losing anther 1.6 jobs on top. For tech, the impact is even more pronounced. Moretti notes that "For each new high-tech job in a city, five additional jobs are ultimately created outside of the high-tech sector in that city, both in skilled occupations (lawyers, teachers, nurses) and in unskilled ones (waiters, hairdressers, carpenters)."[27]

In fact, Moretti argues that "the innovation sector has the largest multiplier of all: about three times larger than that of manufacturing."[28] It is for this reason, that Moretti argues "the best way for a city or state to generate jobs for less skilled workers is to attract high-tech companies that hire highly skilled ones."[29] High-tech workers create jobs across the spectrum.

Kioskification: Robocalypse versus Robotopia

The downside risks of kiosks seemed like a sign of a coming Robocalypse during the trip to New York City I described in Chapter 4. But I see things in a more nuanced way now. Looking at it from an income perspective, wherever there is a demand (or the chance of higher demand), kiosks will be implemented to do work. It is often work that people may not want or could not handle (e.g. selling cupcakes at 3am or selling storing luggage quickly in bins stacked 20 feet high). But, there are still risks. And those are tied to the tax policies I will discuss in the next chapter.

Lots of Freedom, If Not Squandered

In sum, there are three big components of the Robotopia that robots and automation bring to the world:

They free your time.
They free your movement.
They increase your choice of goods and services.

This is the stuff of the *Declaration of Independence*: Life, Liberty, and the Pursuit of Happiness.[30] And yet, it is the U.S. government's own unbalanced books that could end the upside potential for the automation and robotics party, before it even starts. If the Robocalypse hits the labor market, it is likely to occur because of poor government planning and unreformed entitlements obligations that incentivize excessive automation behavior. Kioskification could be one of the brightest spots of the automation age. But, if kioskification and automation are incentivized to an extreme by bad fiscal policies, our story will not end in Robotopia — it will end in Robocalypse.

CHAPTER 6

UNREFORMED ENTITLEMENTS INCENTIVIZE AUTOMATION

Prophets of Robocalypse and Robotopia could debate all day long about the number of jobs robots and automation will create, versus the number of jobs they will destroy. However, one thing that both sides could probably agree on, is that companies respond to tax incentives. And tax incentives are currently structured to incentivize automation beyond what may be sustainable for the overall U.S. economy and labor market. Three key factors have created a perfect storm of tax incentives to drive an acceleration of automation that could crowd out humans:

The U.S. National Debt

Entitlements

Demographics

Without a reform of the entitlement system, increasingly high levels of government debt and changing demographics are likely to contribute to an acceleration of automation — and a reduction of jobs.

The National Debt

The U.S. national debt is a problem, and it is growing. At almost $20 trillion, the national debt is not a small sum. In fact, it comes out to almost $62,000 for every man, woman, and child living in the United States of America.[1] That is a lot of debt!

As you can see in Figure 6-1, the pace at which the U.S. national debt is rising has accelerated. It took 205 years for the U.S. national debt to exceed $1 trillion, which happened in October 1981.[2] But, it then took less than five years for the national debt to double to $2 trillion in April 1986.[3] The most recent doubling of the U.S. national debt occurred over the past eight years, partially as a result of the economic fallout from the Great Recession.[4]

Figure 6-1: Total Federal Debt[5]

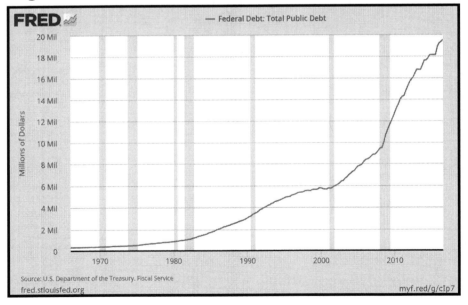

Figure 6-2: Total Federal Debt as a Percent of GDP[6]

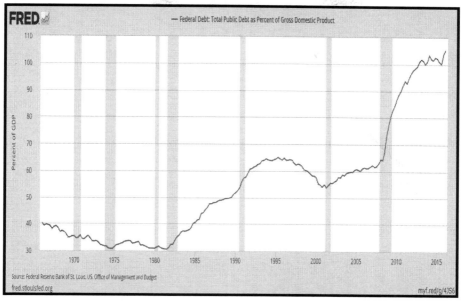

Debt-to-GDP Ratio

Although not as pronounced as the trend in total debt, the debt-to-GDP ratio has risen sharply since the onset of the Great Recession as well (Figure 6-2). One major negative impact of a high national debt, is the drag on potential GDP growth. Plus, compounded debt exposures increase over time, and are exacerbated by interest on the debt.

Unfortunately, while the U.S. national debt is large, the financial situation of U.S. entitlements is much larger — and it is likely to compound U.S. debt problems in coming years. Simply put, entitlements pose the greatest threat to future U.S. government debt levels.

Entitlements

U.S. entitlements include Medicare, Medicaid, and Social Security. And they are financed by payroll taxes from workers. Payroll taxes are separate from income taxes, and while income tax rates could fall if fiscal policies change, payroll taxes are on a one-way trip higher. You see, entitlements are wildly underfunded.

All the sovereign debt in the world totals around 60 trillion dollars.[7] That is the debt cumulatively held by all national governments in the world. But the size of unfunded U.S. entitlements might be more than 2.5 times the size of that level. That's right: the unfunded, off-balance sheet obligations for Medicare, Medicaid, and Social Security could be $200 trillion.[8]

This level of off-balance sheet debt obligation existentially threatens the U.S. economy. The Heritage Foundation has taken calculations from the U.S. Congressional Budget Office about entitlements to create Figure 6-3, which looks quite catastrophic. Basically, by 2030, all U.S. tax revenue will be consumed by entitlements and the interest on the national debt.

While entitlement obligations are a potential disaster looming ahead, the political will to face these challenges is lacking. Entitlement reform is critical for the future of work. Unreformed entitlements present the #1 risk for a Robocalypse in the labor market. Without reform, payroll taxes will rise, and employers, employees, and the self-employed will be disincentivized to work.

Figure 6-3: Tax Revenue Spent on Entitlements[9]

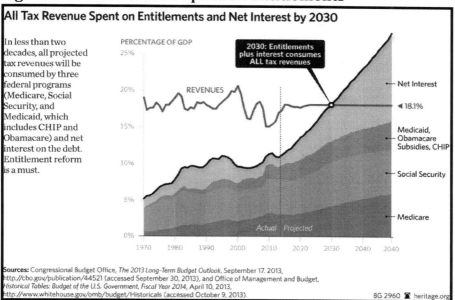

All Tax Revenue Spent on Entitlements and Net Interest by 2030

In less than two decades, all projected tax revenues will be consumed by three federal programs (Medicare, Social Security, and Medicaid, which includes CHIP and Obamacare) and net interest on the debt. Entitlement reform is a must.

PERCENTAGE OF GDP

2030: Entitlements plus interest consumes ALL tax revenues

REVENUES

Net Interest

◄ 18.1%

Medicaid, Obamacare Subsidies, CHIP

Social Security

Medicare

Actual *Projected*

1970   1980   1990   2000   2010   2020   2030   2040   2040

Sources: Congressional Budget Office, *The 2013 Long-Term Budget Outlook*, September 17, 2013, http://cbo.gov/publication/44521 (accessed September 30, 2013), and Office of Management and Budget, *Historical Tables: Budget of the U.S. Government, Fiscal Year 2014*, April 10, 2013, http://www.whitehouse.gov/omb/budget/Historicals (accessed October 9, 2013).

BG 2960 🐘 heritage.org

The Grandfather of U.S. Social Security

Part of the problem with entitlements lies in their origins. The U.S. Social Security Administration website credits Otto von Bismarck as the grandfather of U.S. entitlements. Not LBJ, FDR or Woodrow Wilson, but Bismarck — a Prussian monarchist. Isn't that a dandy anachronism? Neither Prussians nor monarchists are to be found in abundance, but the system Otto created still exists. Bismarck's portrait is even on the U.S. Social Security Administration's website (Figure 6-4).

Bismarck was a powerful politician known for his use of *Realpolitik*, a political doctrine built on pragmatism to advance national self interests. For him, entitlements were convenient and expedient. Unfortunately, that is no longer the case. Today, entitlements threaten to crush the U.S. economy and usher in a labor market Robocalypse.

Bismarck's system was also sustainable. His system guaranteed a pension to German workers over 70. But, the average life expectancy in Germany in the late 1880s was only 40.[10] In other words, so few people were expected to receive the benefits that the program's cost would be negligible.

Figure 6-4: Grandfather of Social Security, Otto von Bismarck[11]

Bismarck rigged entitlements to help crush his political opponents, without having to pay out. But the current entitlement system in the United States is an unfunded liability that threatens to crush the entire economy and usher in a labor market Robocalypse. Plus, fixing entitlements presents a horrible dilemma, as many Americans rely heavily on entitlements for income (Figure 6-5).

Figure 6-5: Importance of Social Security for Income[12]

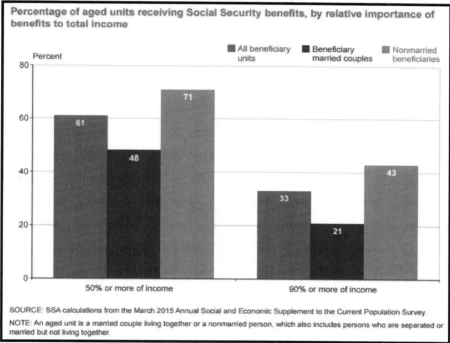

But how did this system break down? Bismarck had such a good thing going. What happened?

This can be answered in one word: demographics.

Demographics

U.S. demographics have slowed sharply, and they are an unstoppable force. As life expectancy has increased, birthrates have also fallen. This compounds the funding shortfalls for entitlements. Worse still: no president, congressman, or governor can change U.S. demographics. This is bigger than one person.

U.S. population growth in the United States has fallen from annual rates of over 1.5 percent per year during the 1950s and early 1960s to just 0.7 percent in the past three years (Figure 6-6). Some of this slowing in population growth is due to a decline in the U.S. fertility rate. In general, fertility rates have been dropping globally, but according to demographer Jonathan Last, the U.S. fertility rate is relatively high at 1.93.[13]

Figure 6-6: Annual Population Growth[14]

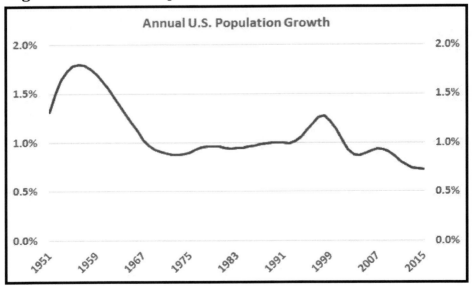

However, even though the U.S. total fertility rate is relatively high compared to other industrialized nations, it is below the 2.1 percent "golden number," which is required to maintain a population, according to Last.[15]

This is a huge problem for maintaining entitlements. After all, the entitlement system worked really well in 1940, when there were 159.4 workers per beneficiary (Figure 6-7), but it is more challenging since that number fell to only 2.8 in 2013. Plus, it is likely to fall to 2 workers per beneficiary by 2040.[16]

Figure 6-7: Ratio of Workers to Social Security Beneficiaries[17]

Year	Covered Workers (in thousands)	Beneficiaries (in thousands)	Ratio
1940	35,390	222	159.4
1945	46,390	1,106	41.9
1950	48,280	2,930	16.5
1955	65,200	7,563	8.6
1960	72,530	14,262	5.1
1965	80,680	20,157	4.0
1970	93,090	25,186	3.7
1975	100,200	31,123	3.2
1980	113,656	35,118	3.2
1985	120,565	36,650	3.3
1990	133,672	39,470	3.4
1995	141,446	43,107	3.3
2000	155,295	45,166	3.4
2005	159,081	48,133	3.3
2010	156,725	53,398	2.9
2013	163,221	57,471	2.8

Entitlements are under siege from both sides, as the birth rate has fallen, and life expectancy has risen. On the one hand, U.S. life expectancy has doubled since Bismarck implemented entitlements in Germany in 1889 — from around 40 years to 80 years. Plus, the age at which people receive entitlements benefits has actually been lowered from 70 to 65. On top of a significantly larger population being eligible to receive entitlements, the medical costs required to support an aging population have risen.

Everything might be ok — if U.S. population growth was extremely robust. But, it is not. Population growth has slowed to less than half the rate seen during the Baby Boom years, and total U.S. fertility rate is below the "golden number" that is required to maintain a population. As Last notes, "Social Security is, in essence, a Ponzi scheme. Like all Ponzi schemes, it works just fine – so long as the intake of new participants continues to increase."[18] Unfortunately, the entitlements program is nearing a breaking point.

Another big problem with slowing birthrates is the manifestation of a shrinking tax base, at the same time that unfunded financial obligations are rising. The unfunded $200 trillion or more in future entitlements payments will be borne by an increasingly smaller proportion of the population.

And as the population ages, there is another issue: who will do the work, as a growing percentage of the population becomes too old to work? The answer is simple: we will create jobs for robots.

Enter the Robots

The dynamics of high debt, massive unfunded entitlements, risks of higher payroll taxes, and a falling birthrate could create the perfect storm to usher in a Robocalypse of the labor market. Automation solves some of the demographic problems we have in the United States, but it threatens to exacerbate some of the entitlement problems. So, as the U.S. population growth slows and older workers age out of the workforce, automation could provide an alternative solution to potential labor shortfalls.

Automation has the potential to contribute significantly to U.S. economic growth and society in a number of ways, as we discussed in Chapter 5. But reconciling the costs associated with unfunded entitlements, will be critical to ensuring automation is orderly and sustainable, rather than an uncontrollable wave of inefficient automation, driven by a desire for employers to avoid paying higher payroll taxes.

Payroll Taxes for Robots?

Some thought leaders have proposed putting payroll taxes on robots.[19] This seems complicated and potentially less effective (although easier) than reforming entitlements. Still, where would we draw the line?

Would there be a justification to charge payroll taxes on automated vehicles? Should companies pay payroll taxes on mining and construction equipment? And what about computers? I discuss the risks of this tax further in Chapter 7.

Accelerating a Reduction in the U.S. Tax Base

Slowing population growth and the need to automate more jobs is likely to exacerbate debt and entitlement problems, by accelerating the reduction in the U.S. tax base, especially for payroll taxes, which fund entitlements. After all, if entitlements obligations cannot be met with current funding, payroll taxes will rise.

And who pays payroll taxes?

Employees split entitlements costs with their employers, who pay half. This means that if entitlements costs rise, the cost for an employer to keep a person employed increases. The substitution effect of automation for labor is going to accelerate, because of the financial incentives in place for employers.

As payroll taxes increase to cover the costs associated with underfunded entitlements, the financial incentives for employers to shift work away from human laborers, and add technology, is likely to be reinforced. A number of my clients have shared their concerns about the risk of rising costs associated with healthcare costs for their workers.

How do you think employers will feel about the burden of paying much higher payroll taxes? They do pay half of them, after all.

As automation increases, there is likely to be an increasing incentive for employers to automate even more, since robots will unlikely be part of the entitlements tax base, and additional automation will pose further upside risks for employer payroll tax obligations. This will shrink the entitlements tax base further.

Given these dynamics, an acceleration in automation exacerbates entitlement funding issues. It becomes a dragon chasing its tail. Like the PSA from 1980 about doing cocaine to work longer to make more money, to buy more cocaine, to work longer, to make more money, to buy more cocaine.[20] Except for the United States, the addiction isn't cocaine, its unfunded entitlements that rest on unsound fundamentals, stretching back to a Prussian monarchist.

This is the same problem of "feeding the dragon" that has hurt numerous industries with defined benefits plans for their employees, like autos and airlines. Entitlements are also defined benefits plans, but they don't threaten one industry with bankruptcy; they threaten the entire U.S. economy.

Private company defined benefits plans, as well as public city and state employee pension funds, were modeled on demographic structures that used to be much more favorable and sustainable for the pensions in place. These same challenges threaten U.S. entitlements. And, of course, any industry, company, or government entity with defined benefits plans.

Kioskification Revisited

Unreformed entitlements present a significant risk of over-automation to the U.S. economy. If you were to think of the most important benefits you get as an employee, you might think of time off or sick days. But your employer probably thinks about the most expensive items first: payroll taxes and health care. Kiosks don't get time off, and they certainly don't require health care or payroll taxes — for now.

In mid-2016, unemployment in Spain was around 20 percent[21] and youth unemployment was around 43 percent.[22] So, there were a lot of people available to work. But, in Figure 6-8, you see kiosks that were hard at work in Barcelona, Spain during the summer of 2016. In Spain, as in much of Europe, the cost to hire someone can be prohibitive, compared to the United States. And these kiosks require no payroll taxes, no health insurance costs, no government entitlements, no vacation, no sick days, and no union problems. With these kinds of kiosks replacing workers, youth unemployment is unlikely to get significantly better. This also bodes ill for U.S. youth participation and unemployment rates. Be advised, fast food robots are coming.

Increases in the U.S. minimum wage are beneficial for workers receiving those wages. But they are detrimental if no one actually receives those wages. Higher minimum wages in Los Angeles, for example, hastened the arrival of robots to do minimum wage jobs.[23] And higher wages will have an even greater total labor cost to employers, when payroll taxes rise. This could compound the drive toward automation and kioskification for employers wishing to avoid higher total labor costs

Figure 6-8: Jobs For Robots in Barcelona.[24]

Entrepreneurs at Risk

Rising entitlement costs and payroll taxes could also stifle entrepreneurship. Unlike employees, who split payroll tax obligations with their employers, self-employed people bear the full brunt of payroll taxes personally. The rate is currently 15.3 percent of income.[25] In the future, that rate will rise faster for entrepreneurs, since they will not be splitting the increase in payroll taxes with an employer. If entitlements are not drastically overhauled, a self-employment tax rate of 25 percent by 2030 is not inconceivable.

Increasingly high self-employment tax rates are likely to stifle entrepreneurship and hurt self-employed workers. According to an article by the Pew Foundation, the percent of employed workers who are self employed fell from 11.4 percent in 1990 to 10 percent in 2014.[26] More importantly, the Pew Foundation notes that 30 percent of U.S. jobs are held "by the self-employed and the workers they hire."[27] In other words, in 2014, 14.6 million self-employed workers hired another 29.4 million workers, making 30 percent of employees.

With the prospect of entitlement shortfalls, and a shrinking tax base, self-employment tax rates are going to rise. The impact of these additional costs is likely to engender a continued downward trend in the percent of self-employed workers. Plus, workers in the so-called "gig economy" — like all 1099s — are also subject to self-employment taxes. This could make the existence of the gig economy less tenable, as payroll taxes rise.

Other Unfunded Obligations

Consider also that the $200 trillion figure for unfunded entitlements does not take into account the scary pension data for federal, state, county, or city government employees. Many of these workers also have defined benefits pensions that are underfunded and in great need of reform. The gap in funds for these pensions will also likely incentivize automation and drive jobs for robots — rather than people.

Summary

There is an old joke that the best kind of auto worker to be is a retired auto worker. Without a reform of entitlements, the joke could be that the best kind of any U.S. worker to be will be a retired U.S. worker. This will affect all of us, since unfunded off-balance sheet obligations could necessitate that benefits be drastically reduced (especially for future generations), while contribution costs rise further. Problems beget problems.

Automation incentivized by tax requirements as a result of unreformed entitlements present a deal with the devil. After all, automation financially incentivized by risks of increased payroll taxes, increased healthcare costs, and higher minimum wage rates, could contribute to problems in these areas. Automation accelerates and exacerbates the problems of a national defined benefits program (e.g. entitlements) that worked best when the age at which one received benefits exceeded life expectancy by 30 years. Robots and automation can solve the shrinking population problem, but they exacerbate the problem of a shrinking tax base, especially for entitlements and underfunded pensions.

CHAPTER 7

PROBLEMS WITH
UNIVERSAL BASIC INCOME

Universal basic income (UBI) is the notion that everyone will be paid a flat salary regardless of whether they work or not. And the biggest problem with universal basic income, is that we simply cannot afford it. As you saw in the previous chapter, U.S. entitlement obligations, which could be as high as $200 trillion, make a further expansion of U.S. budgetary obligations for UBI virtually impossible.

According to David Freedman, who wrote an article on the subject for *MIT Technology Review*, an annual payment of $10,000 to every adult American "would be at least twice as expensive as current antipoverty benefits and overhead, adding between one and two trillion dollars to federal budget."[1] Furthermore, Freedman argues that "existing safety-net programs could be expanded and tuned to eliminate poverty about as effectively but much less expensively, and they could continue to focus on providing jobs and the incentives to take them."[2] In other words, the inefficient programs in place could be better than UBI. Yikes!

Risks Beyond Cost

Aside from the cost of UBI, which is insurmountable, there are four major problems with UBI:

Inflation would rise.

Taxes would rise.

Long-term economic development could be stifled.

Society could become fractured.

European Attitudes

In Figure 7-1, you can see the results of a recent survey, in which Europeans voiced support for universal basic income. However, despite this support, UBI has so far failed when voters went to the ballot box to vote on the idea. As such, no individual nations have voted to approve this policy.

The entire concept of UBI smacks of full blown communism, with a redistribution of income. Perhaps this is why Europeans, who have a more colorful political history than Americans, find it to be an appealing option. However, it is more likely that UBI finds support in Europe, because the same respondents who support UBI, do not actually know what it is. This is shown in Figure 7-2.

I wager that graphs of European opinions and knowledge about communism during the 1920s may have looked somewhat similar. For my European friends, as well as my American ones, let us now consider some costs of UBI that go beyond the budget.

Figure 7-1: Europeans Who Would Vote for Basic Income[3]

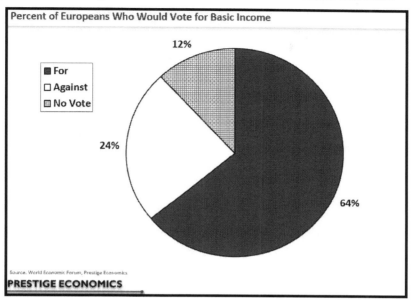

Figure 7-2: Europeans Familiar with Basic Income[4]

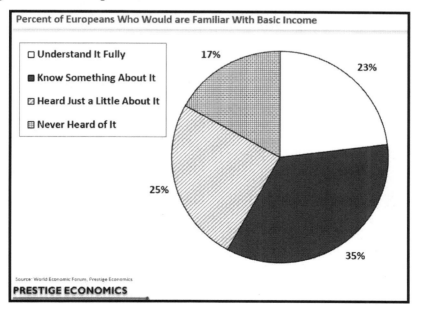

Inflation

Inflation is when prices rise and the dollars you have lose purchasing power. In other words, prices get inflated, and the value of the dollars you own goes down. There has been a secular decline in rates of year-over-year inflation in the United States, since it peaked in June 1979, as you can see in Figure 7-3.

Now, imagine for a second, what would happen if everyone got UBI? This is basically free money and everyone gets it. What would happen to the price of a cup of coffee, a car, clothes, or food, if every single adult received a handout from the government for doing nothing? How much is a Honda, when everyone is handed half a Honda in free income for doing nothing every year?

Figure 7-3: U.S. Consumer Price Inflation Rate[5]

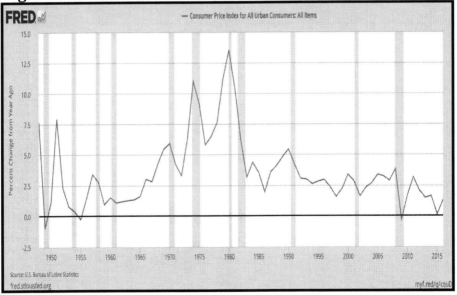

The logical outcome seems pretty straightforward: prices would rise. Higher rates of inflation are good for asset holders and debt holders, but they are particularly bad for people on fixed income.

Fixed income investments include corporate bonds and Treasuries, as well as Social Security and defined benefits pension payments. Given the risk of inflation from UBI, the minute people get UBI income and begin spending it, prices would rise and those fixed income payments would be devalued.

As prices rise, the need to increase UBI would also rise. This would, in turn, send prices even higher, justifying the need to further increase UBI. And so forth and so on. So how much is enough? The truth is that once we go down the path of UBI, no amount may be enough. The printing presses of the future will need to digitally issue new money for UBI at an ever-quickening pace.

Low, stable inflation is conducive to growth, and high levels of inflation can make an economy unstable. If prices rise rapidly, as they did in Germany in the hyperinflation of the early 1920s, people could end up wallpapering their homes with worthless paper currency. To use a more recent example, paper bills could be denominated in the trillions, like they are in Zimbabwe.

Now, I'm not saying UBI would put us on the same path as 1920s Germany or modern-day Zimbabwe.

But I'm not saying it won't.

Taxes Would Rise

Since we cannot afford to pay for UBI with our current government budget, and we cannot afford to drive up our national debt by another 1 to 2 trillion dollars (in today's value) annually, we would need to find the money for UBI somewhere else. We could just print it, but that means running up the debt; we can't surreptitiously run dollar printing presses, sneaking bags of UBI into everyone's home while they sleep like some kind of income Santa. But that is likely the plan most people are going with. Better stock up on milk and cookies now!

But in all seriousness, there is only one way to get the money we need for UBI: taxes. It could be higher payroll taxes, higher corporate taxes, higher property taxes, or the creation of some new taxes, like a robotic labor payroll tax. But one thing is certain: taxes will rise.

I mention something in Chapter 6 that we can agree on: corporations (and individuals) respond to tax incentives. And higher taxes that are implemented to purely redistribute wealth without any labor or activity requirement on the part of the recipient would reduce incentives for technological development, investment, and economic activity.

Payroll Taxes on Robots

The debate about a payroll tax on robots is heating up, and a number of business leaders, including Bill Gates, have voiced support for such a policy. But defining which jobs are affected will be a challenge. Would it be for robots *and* computers?

The debate over a robot payroll tax is unlikely to go away, but its implementation, and the allocation of associated tax revenues, could be complicated. But a robot payroll tax is likely to be something that policymakers look at more closely over time, especially if a high number of jobs are automated out of existence.

Of course, the money from a robot payroll tax *could* be earmarked to fulfill the unfunded entitlement obligations of Medicare, Medicaid, and Social Security. After all, these are already funded by payroll taxes. But, even with a robot payroll tax, policymakers may neglect to fund entitlement obligations, because if robot payroll taxes go to fund entitlements, there may not be much wiggle room to implement UBI.

Although I am very skeptical of the concepts of a robot payroll tax and universal basic income, one thing in the world of politics always rings true: when you rob Peter to pay Paul, you can always count on Paul's vote. In this case, Paul would be a robot without a vote. And Peter would get free money.

Corporate Taxes

At the time this book was going to print, there was a hot debate about tax reform, including lowering corporate taxes. A move in the future to significantly raise corporate taxes to finance the UBI free handout for every American would likely meet with sharp resistance — and corporate relocations. Our economy could experience a mass exodus of corporations that would seek to avoid UBI taxation. They would just leave.

Of course, we could single out technology corporations, but as noted previously, technology companies have a 5x multiplier on job creation. Want to see the UBI needs balloon quickly? Scare away companies, where each job they create is capable of supporting the creation of five additional jobs.

Taxes on Income Assets

Another way to finance UBI would be to tax people who work. Yes, everyone gets free UBI money. But, the people who also get paid to work, will pay for everyone else to get the UBI money — even if none of the other recipients work, want to work, ever plan to work, or if the other UBI recipients just want to play some future virtual reality holodeck version of Xbox their entire lives. This leads us to our next topic, and the negative risks to long-term economic development from implementing such a UBI system.

Death and Taxes — or at Least Taxes

Before closing out this section, I want to note that there are currently two guarantees in life: death and taxes. Singulatarians and Transhumanists, like Zoltan Istvan, would tell you that death is not guaranteed in the future. In the future you may be able to live forever. However, taxes are still going to be guaranteed. And with the implementation of UBI, *higher* taxes would also be guaranteed.

Negative Long-Run Economic Impacts

Think back to Chapter 2, the chapter about names and medieval occupations. During the industrial revolution — at the onset of the age of iron and steel — factories decimated the occupations of smiths, weavers, and many others.

Of course, there were very unpleasant times during the industrial revolution. There were widespread abuses of the labor force, including child labor, horrific working conditions, and a lack of worker protection. This led to the creation of unions, and resulted in labor reforms. Things like weekends, holidays, and paid vacations came from the development of unions, and a push towards more humane working environments. The problems may have been imperfectly fixed, but society improved, and the economy progressed.

At the same time that village life was fully eroding, the emergence and creation of new professions also became critical. And broader access to university-level education helped train more doctors, journalists, lawyers, and other professionals. And there were great improvements across a number of professions and industries, which had very positive impacts on society. But, what would have happened if people had just stayed in their villages and they had just been given a handout?

Medieval Universal Basic Income

Imagine in the 1800s, if European monarchs decided to just hand out money to smiths, millers, and weavers to never work again. What would have happened to European growth? What if these tradesmen managed to wrangle UBI out of the U.S. government in the late 1800s? What would have happened to the U.S. economy?

I suspect that such policies would have caused economies to suffer from significant underperformance, stifled economic development, and slow growth.

With such negative ramifications, why are people talking about UBI now?

UBI does not help individuals bridge skills gaps. It just avoids the problem by throwing money at it. But in doing so, it short circuits the adaptive nature of capitalist economies, and it reduces the longer-term potential for economic growth. This is something we need to think about in relation to UBI. If everyone just got a handout, the economy will stop adapting — it will stop growing.

More importantly, there is an individual cost to UBI as a solution to permanent job loss. If individuals in the late 1800s were given money because their jobs ceased to exist — because society has changed, what would have happened to those individual smiths, millers, tanners, and weavers, if they did nothing? Would they have also felt that they were nothing? What would have happened to society at that point?

What will happen to ours, if people do nothing and receive UBI?

German Shepherds

While a number of jobs over time are going to change and become obsolete, I fundamentally believe that humans will need things to do, and that lives of leisure are not exactly lives of pure contentment. Yes, a lot of years of leisure is nice. But, have you ever wondered why billionaires continue to work? It's because they are German Shepherds.

Most people I know — my family, close friends, and even acquaintances — remind me of German Shepherds. They like to have things to do. They like to be busy and occupied. Anyone who has ever owned a German Shepherd, watched a German Shepherd, or volunteered in an animal shelter, knows that if these dogs don't have enough to do, they'll destroy the furniture in their own house, out of sheer boredom. It is my fundamental belief, that people without enough to do will also rip up their own lives just to avoid being bored.

This is also the lesson of Greek mythology. Greek gods and goddesses got into wars and conflicts because they were bored. With nothing to do, they wreaked havoc on the world for no reason other than sheer boredom. We should be concerned.

It's one thing when retirees receive entitlements, because they are generally less physically active. But, it's another thing entirely, when young adults are unoccupied; they need things to do. This could be a challenge in a future with more robots and automation. Without a way to keep people mentally and physically active, there are risks to society. It is a threat that people don't often talk about.

Idle hands are the work of the devil. For this reason, it is going to be a very big problem, if people don't have something to do. A world without work — a world of UBI — presents existential risks to society.

As Kaplan pointed out in his book on robots and the future of work, *Humans Need Not Apply*, "Money is not the only reason to work. People like to feel that they are useful members of society. They enjoy making a contribution to the welfare of others in addition to providing for themselves and their families. Most people feel great satisfaction in helping others, increasing their sense of self-worth, and giving their lives purpose and meaning."[6]

Figure 7-4: Busy People are Happy People[9]

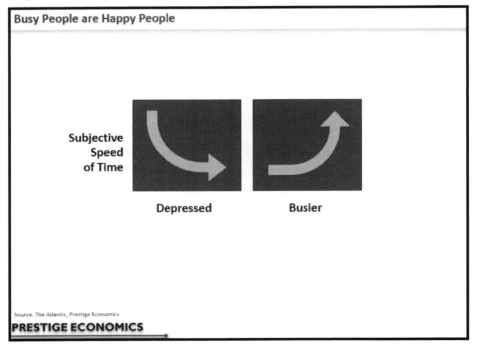

I have long said that busy people are happy people, which was a concept reinforced by an article in *The Atlantic* from February 2017, including Figure 7-4.[7] Another *The Atlantic* writer noted that "The paradox of work is that many people hate their jobs, but they are considerably more miserable doing nothing."[8]

The Grandfather of Universal Basic Income

When the Berlin Wall fell in 1989 and the Soviet Union subsequently collapsed in 1991, the West declared that capitalism had defeated communism. But, the view of history changes with time. After all, it is now accepted by most historians of European history that World War I and World War II were one war with a lengthy armistice between two periods of actual armed conflict. I must then wonder if we have actually seen the end of communism, or if we are merely lodged in a period of armistice.

After all, if universal basic income makes it across the finish line of history, we may come to view the "end" of the Cold War as just Round One of a struggle that capitalism could yet lose. I have read the works of communist leaders: Marx, Engels, Lenin, Luxemburg, and Trotsky. But some of their writings are less aggressive than the language used by some Silicon Valley futurists when they speak about a post-capitalist Robotopia. Make no mistake: the final judgement on the failure of communism may not yet have been written. And while Bismarck is considered the grandfather of U.S. social security, I think we need to recognize that Karl Marx would be the grandfather of universal basic income.

Figure 7-5: Grandfather of Universal Basic Income, Karl Marx[10]

Universal Basic Income is Not a Viable Choice

The costs of universal basic income are high. UBI could lead to rampant inflation, an exodus of businesses, higher taxes, long-term economic stagnation, and a fracturing of individuals and society. Universal basic income is not a viable choice. We must adapt to the coming changes. Fortunately, as you will see in the next chapter, we are better prepared to do so than ever before.

UBI proponents could say: *"Non-workers of the world unite!"*

CHAPTER 8

THE FUTURE OF EDUCATION

The answer to technological unemployment is not the long-term handout of universal basic income. The answer is education. Education is both the greatest weapon we have against Robocalypse, and it is the best tool with which we can equip our population to be productive and engaged members of society. Leveraging the democratization of online education to provide opportunities for workers will be critical, as the information age catapults us into the automation age.

In this chapter, I will share some information about changes going on in the field of education. For example, in some cases, the physical classroom that has moved online, is now an in-hand classroom with a television studio on the backend. Thanks to robots, your next class could be in-hand, rather than on campus.

Then, in Chapter 9, I will discuss evergreen professional opportunities, the importance of constantly learning, and the value of massive online job postings to discover greater professional opportunities for success than ever before.

It's Not East Being Green

A green room is a room where people relax or prepare to go on television — or be video recorded. And I have seen a lot of green rooms in my life; I've done a lot of TV. Some green rooms are beautifully decked out with a wall of televisions, fish tanks, and treats. They're also sometimes filled with celebrities. I have shared green rooms with Karl Rove, Michael Eisner, and Travis Kalanick, the CEO of Uber.

Of all the green rooms that I've seen, and of all the cool green room stories I have, there is one green room that blew my mind above all others. It was the green room of the University of Texas, at Austin in Figure 8-1. That's right, UT Austin has a green room. It used to be a teacher's lounge, or a classroom, or a language lab. Now, it's where professors put on makeup before going on camera in front of hundreds or thousands of students.

Figure 8-1: University of Texas at Austin Green Room[1]

As UT's online education course offerings have expanded, so has the space taken over by production teams, including a green room. UT Austin has a mandate to significantly increase the number of classes they offer online. Effectively, they are trying to remove bottlenecks in their education system by putting more classes for general education requirements online, so more students graduate in a timely fashion.

The Rise of MOOCs

Like many universities, The University of Texas is riding the wave of online education. And it's a wave that isn't going down. In Figure 8-2, you can see how total global Massive Open Online Courses (MOOCs) have grown. Some of UT's courses are Simultaneous Massive Online Courses (SMOCs).

Figure 8-2: Global Growth of MOOCs [2]

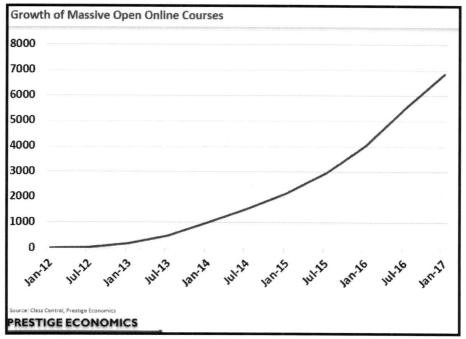

There are some critical differences between SMOCs and MOOCs. SMOCs require students to be online at the same time as the course. MOOCs have generally been free, but that appears to be changing, with some education platforms now charging fees.

Aside from general education course requirements, entire Bachelor's, Master's, and Doctoral degrees have gone completely online. Online education opportunities have increased significantly over the past five years, and they are poised to increase further. I personally completed a Master's degree online, and I would recommend it to anyone. It might not be my last.

Online learning is so hot that futurist Thomas Frey expects by "2030 the largest company on the internet is going to be an education-based company that we haven't heard of yet."3 But futurist, Jeremy Rifkin, expects something very different. He sees the U.S. economy moving in the direction of a society where everything has "'near zero' marginal cost" — where everything is nearly free.4 And he expects "learning in online virtual classrooms at near zero marginal cost, [will bring] the economy into an era of nearly free goods and services."5

Having taken online courses, I'm with Frey on this one. Instead of a limited number of students in a physical classroom, thousands of students can take a course online. Eventually, hundreds of thousands of people could take the same course. But there are administrative costs to formal education. And people will pay to learn, because they know there is a positive return on investment to education. As such, online education will grow as an industry. And it might be a very long time before formal education is free.

Figure 8-3: University of Texas at Austin Green Screen[6]

Unlike a green room, the UT room with a green screen is used for interesting and fun editing in images and backgrounds.

If you don't need an office, you don't need a physical classroom.

Think about expensive, often ostentatious, real estate of a university and the growing number of people globally and domestically who want to attend American universities. You don't necessarily need to keep building more campuses, if people can attend remotely. In the same way that you can buy a ticket to see a baseball game without a season tickets, you also don't need to attend every class in person to boast that you went to a certain university. In content-centric subjects, to say that you have a degree from somewhere is just as good as if you were there just once — or there for every single class

Like a sitcom from the 1980s, UT Austin has a live studio audience for some of their courses. In Figure 8-4, you can see where a studio audience for some of the UT Austin online courses sits. Each seat has a microphone with which students can ask questions. In some cases, seats are allocated in advance.

In Figure 8-5, you can see the three-camera shot from the audience perspective. This is a high production value recording set up: green room, room with green screen, audience seating, three-camera shot, professional tech, and post-production on the back end.

Online courses have tremendous value. However, I believe there is likely to be a bifurcation of value for degrees going forward. For some degrees, networking will be critical, but for other degrees this could prove irrelevant.

Figure 8-4: Filmed Before a Live Studio Audience[7]

Figure 8-5: Three-Camera Shot[8]

Business Degrees

Undergraduate business degrees and MBAs are going to continue to derive a high value from direct human contact with other students. Networking and personal relationships contribute significantly to the value of a degree when studying business, because those relationships foster the creation of near-term and long-term professional opportunities. There is no substitute for in-person relationships in the business world.

Of course, in addition to networking, business students can derive significant value from gaining project management skills and financial acumen. Those skills should augment opportunities significantly in the future.

Non-Business Degrees

For other graduate (and undergraduate) degrees, however, networking isn't as important. If you are going to become a teacher, a nurse, or an IT professional, you don't necessarily need to be physically in a classroom to derive the greatest benefit of your degree. You need to learn the content, but you don't necessarily need the network as much as you do in business.

Some professions have a very easy funnel, in terms of getting you into a job. In areas where there are labor shortfalls, like healthcare, if you have the right qualification, you should land something pretty quickly. This is why the networking of an in-person degree is less important for some careers. However, if you plan to have a long career in any kind of managerial capacity, networking is absolutely everything. You should skip the actual classes before you decide to skip the networking!

Tales of Three Master's Degrees

Reduced human contact in an online course represents a significant loss of value for some degrees. But, it very much depends on what you are studying. Let me share my own experiences from three very different graduate school programs.

For my Master's in German literature at the University of North Carolina at Chapel Hill, the content was the most critical component of my work. Although I enjoyed the discussions, I actually read most of my books for the entire school year during the summers before my first and second years of grad school. In isolation, I read all of the material for my classes. It was not quite distance, but I completed almost everything remotely. I could have done this just fine remotely — especially since I was living in Germany speaking the language constantly.

For my Master's of Applied Economics and MBA coursework at the University of North Carolina at Greensboro, the content was important, but getting to know my classmates was even more important. Because it was a business program, the networking contributed to my personal and professional success.

For my Master's of Negotiation at CSU Dominguez Hills, the content was the most critical component of my work. I never went to campus once, and I defended my Master's via Skype. But, I also read over 200 negotiation books in 18 months. It was a great self-directed learning process. If you want the content and structure of an online degree, I would recommend anyone go for it. But, for business degrees, there is no substitute for meeting real people.

More Education Leads to More Money

As we saw in Chapter 4, jobs with low levels of education are most exposed to automation. And those jobs that required graduate degrees has a zero percent chance of automation. Education is a critical equalizer for income and employment.

As you can see in Figure 8-6, the greatest payout is for a Doctorate or professional degree, which is more than double the national average for all education. A Bachelor's comes in second, with Master's degrees a close third. But the entry-level wages from the education of an Associate's degree and higher are all above the overall average.

Figure 8-6: Wages by Entry-Level Education Required[9]

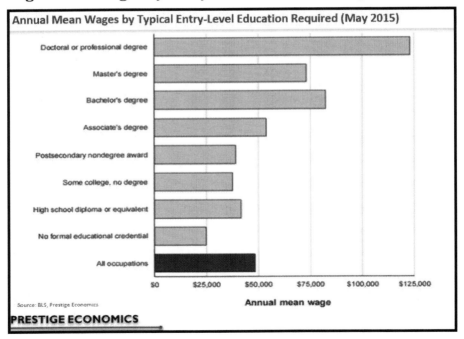

Figure 8-7: Unemployment Rate by Education[10]

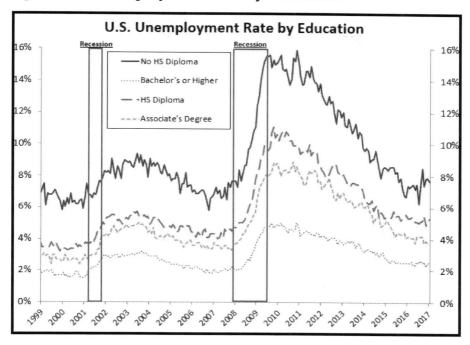

U.S. Unemployment Rate by Education

Unemployment Rate

Education is also inversely correlated with unemployment: the more education you have, the less likely you are to be unemployed — especially during a recession.

In Figure 8-7, you can see the impact of education on unemployment during the Great Recession (shown as a wide recession box), when the unemployment rate increased for all education levels. However, workers without a high school diploma experienced the greatest rise in unemployment, from a low of 5.8 percent in October 2006 to 15.9 percent in November 2010 — a jump of over 10 full percentage points.[11]

Conversely, Figure 8-7 also shows that workers with Bachelor's degrees were much more insulated from the Great Recession, when their unemployment rates rose from a low of 1.8 percent in March 2007 to a high of only 5 percent in September 2009.[12]

It's interesting to note that the worst year for people with a Bachelor's degree was still better than the best year for those without a high school diploma.

Education in Context

In this chapter, as in previous chapters, it should be clear that education and skills are critical defining factors of economic opportunity for individuals. Increasing access to education over time will play a crucial part in determining how the entire economy — and society — develop during the age of automation. Education will be critical for staving off Robocalypse, for mitigating the downside risks from lost opportunities in exposed industries, and for minimizing the impact of technological unemployment in our society. Formal or informal, online or in person, professional or trade: all forms of education improve individuals' job prospects, income levels, and robot-proof status.

The robots are coming, and the safest place to be isn't a bomb shelter, bunker, or deserted island: it's a school.

CHAPTER 9

ROBOT-PROOF YOUR CAREER

You need to prepare for the acceleration of automation and robotics. You need to be robot-proof. But to be on the right side of these changes, you need a strategy to lay the groundwork of your own Robotopia.

There are three main strategies you can implement to prepare for the inevitable disruption of the labor force by automation:

Work in an Evergreen Industry: *Gain professional exposure to a career that will be in demand in the automation age.*

Learn Valuable Skills: *Take advantage of formal and informal education opportunities. Be prepared to learn more.*

Keep Moving: *Put yourself in a position to find opportunities, by changing industries, companies, or geographies.*

In this chapter, I will give examples of these strategies to help you find upside, even if there are downturns in certain industries.

Strategy #1: Work in an Evergreen Industry

No matter how big the economic or automation risks, there are always some industries that will be evergreen. Make sure you have professional exposure to one of them.

The prospect of Robocalypse presents significant uncertainty for a number of industries, especially manufacturing and transportation. Meanwhile, other industries have a relatively low potential for automation. These include jobs in information technology, healthcare, and management. I discussed these dynamics in Chapter 4, and a full list of different industry exposures to automation can be seen in Figure 4-1.

Information Technology

Obviously, increased automation, robotics, and reliance on technology present significant opportunities for careers in the information technology space.

I recently had a call with a former colleague and good friend who works for a company at the forefront of vehicle automation. I was talking to him about the risks to the economy and financial markets. He was very concerned, because part of his compensation is tied to the performance of the NASDAQ.

I told him, "You have nothing to worry about." Then, he asked me why. I was laughing as I told him, "The stock market may fall, but you're going to be the last guy on earth with a job. Literally. The. Last. Guy. It's your job to automate every other job out of existence. You're going to be just fine!"

He was happy with that answer, and if you can find a gig in automation, you'd probably be pretty happy with your prospects too.

By the way, I have followed my own advice about gaining professional exposure to automation. In fact, my company, Prestige Economics, performs extensive research and data analysis for MHI, the material handling industry and trade organization in the United States. This is a multi-billion dollar industry that provides the physical equipment and technology that moves goods through the U.S. supply chain. These are the unsung heroes meeting the rising e-commerce needs of the U.S. economy.

Material handling also happens to be an industry that, in part, is focused on automation, robotics, last mile solutions, and transportation optimization. I have often joked that if my friend doing automated vehicle work will be the last guy on earth with a job, I'm just trying to be the second-to-last guy on earth with a job. The truth is, however, a bit more nuanced, as there are other critical industries that will also be difficult to automate, like healthcare.

Healthcare Jobs

Healthcare is likely to remain evergreen in a world of automation, since it is a more difficult sector to automate, and it involves high levels of human contact. In Chapter 3, I discussed the current state of (and near-term outlook for) the U.S. labor market. And healthcare came up a big winner for near-term job growth, job numbers, and top-end income.

If you are worried about automation, any industry where you need person-to-person contact is likely to remain relatively safe. Generally speaking, health care professions are likely to pay better than other high-contact service sector jobs like hairdressers, estheticians, and massage therapists.

Careers in health care are likely to be solid for a long time to come, since the demographics of an aging U.S. population will necessitate expanding the ranks of front-line healthcare professionals: personal care aides, registered nurses, and home health aides top the list. In Chapter 3 (Figure 3-10), I presented information about the positive outlook for healthcare job growth. The current distribution of jobs in healthcare can be seen in Figure 9-1.

Figure 9-1: Employment in Healthcare[1]

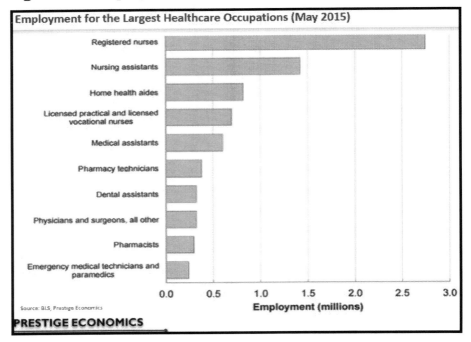

Project Management

As more tasks become automated, project and process management will become increasingly important. With an increasing number of potential uses of automation, the effective prioritization, optimization, and implementation of tasks will be required in order to ensure the highest dollarized value of automation.

In the same way that word processors have necessitated that all professionals develop typing and secretarial skills, professionals of the future will need to have the project management skills of an MBA. Project management skills are even likely to exceed numeracy in importance. After all, even if robots can perform tasks and processes can be automated, it will be a very long time before they will be able to do this without guidance.

And that is where people come into the picture. If robots are doing all of the work, people are going to need to gain project management skills. Because people will need to manage the robots. There are three types of project management that people are already doing, but will need to do more of in the future:

Managing People — telling people which processes to implement in what order.

Managing Robots — telling robots which processes to implement in what order.

Managing People Who Manage Robots — telling the people what the top priorities are, so that they can tell the robots how to prioritize their workflow.

Without an ethical guidance system, and without an understanding of subjective corporate prioritizations, people will be a critical part of the puzzle for some time to come. Robots can get things done, but only if instructed properly.

Surely, you have been in meetings and thought; why can't this just get done? It's like asking for directions, only to be told that you can't get there from here. To answer questions, to get things done, people need to be involved to help identify what the real question is, how to formulate that question, and how to make sure the question is not misspecified. Essentially, we all become MBAs. We all become management consultants. Execution goes to the robots. Planning, prioritizing, allocating resources, and directing activities remain with the humans.

Microentrepreneurs

Maybe IT, healthcare, and management are not for you. What then? Well, as the line from the film *The Untouchables* goes, "if you do not like the apples in the barrel, go pick one off the tree."

Disruption creates opportunity, and there are more opportunities than ever to start your own business. This is especially true at a time when the offices of today are risk of becoming the museums of tomorrow. There has been an emergence of the so-called "gig economy." As Arun Sundararajan, a professor at New York University states in his book, *The Sharing Economy*, that there is potential for a rise of "microentrepreneur[s]...self-employed workers who are empowered to work whenever they want from any location and at whatever level of intensity needed to achieve their desired standard of living."[2]

These new opportunities to be a microentrepreneur are supported by changes that also present greater chances for business owners to connect with the global capital markets than at any other time in history. Although Sundararajan writes that "crowd-based capitalism is still in its infancy,"[3] increased capital market access from crowdfunding presents significant opportunities. People can turn hobbies into businesses by accessing the world via e-commerce and in-hand retail.

There are challenges for this new and relatively untested initiative. And the future of crowdfunding and microentrepreneurs will depend heavily on investment profitability and liquidity. Investors will need to see that their privately-held crowdfunding investments can generate a return and that they can be easily sold in a secondary marketplace. If those hurdles can be jumped, then there will be a lot more opportunities for "the little guy" to access global markets to build a business.

It is now easier to reach an international market and access capital than ever before. If you ever dreamed of being a business owner, now might a good time to go for it! Before you go down that path, however, you might want to check out my book *Recession-Proof* for some of the most important secrets about the process and math behind starting and building a business.

Strategy #2: Learn Valuable Skills

As you read in Chapter 8, access to educational opportunities are much greater than any other time in history. There are also a number of things you can do to enhance and add to your professional skill set to robot-proof yourself.

If you don't have time for a degree, get a certification. There's been huge growth in the number of professional designations available. I have a bunch of letters after my name, and other serious professionals do, too. These build skills, but they are also signaling devices. They signal to a future boss or client that you have knowledge, as well as drive, follow-through, and hunger.

Is there a particular computer program that you'd like to add to your resume? Download the free trial. The 30 days you'll get with that product is more than enough to learn the basics. Then add it to your resume. To include that skill on your resume, you don't need to be the world's expert on that product. Unless that computer program is a critical component of a job, you probably just need to have a basic competence and familiarity with the program, since most companies will train you once you are hired.

Audit a class at your local university. That means showing up to the lectures without being enrolled. You don't get credit or a grade, but you do gain the knowledge, and you can list it on your resume. At many universities, it's free. At others, there's a modest fee. The University of Texas at Austin, charges just $20 to audit an entire class—and that's at one of the country's top public universities. If you want to build your business skills, accounting or finance classes would be good options.

Strategy #3: Keep Moving

Making sure that your education and skills are matched to a solid professional opportunity is critical. It might require you to switch fields, relocate geographically, or just switch companies. Fortunately, you have some of the greatest tools in history available to more easily make those transitions.

In-Hand Labor Market

There have been major changes in the way people look for work in recent years. At the dawn of the industrial revolution, if you lost your job, the only options were to ask the other people in your village for a job. Then, during the industrial revolution, you could have consulted a newspaper for listings. That remained relatively unchanged as the main source of job leads from the mid-1800s until around 2000, when job postings came online. Today, there are about 27 million new U.S. job postings per year, with 5 million online job postings online at any time.[4] Plus, companies like Indeed.com, boast 20 million postings worldwide.

Can you imagine being stuck with whatever job openings happened to be in your hamlet, as opposed to being able to access 20 million job listings all over the world? And the number of job postings online, as well as our access to them, is only likely to increase over time. You now have a full in-hand labor market.

Plus, in the twelve months through December 2016, about 38 percent of workers experienced turnover.[5] Automation could accelerate the frequency of turnover. But the good news is, if you aren't happy, at least you are unlikely to be stuck in a job forever.

We are Ready

One of the most important things about working is that it creates a purpose for people. People derive their identities from their profession, but careers and professions change over time. Although jobs will be constantly changing in coming decades, people are far less tied to their occupations now as an identity that they were when the industrial revolution started.

Interestingly, the main three strategies I have proposed in this chapter are essentially the same strategies I would have given smiths and millers at the dawn of the industrial age:

Work in an Evergreen Industry

Learn Valuable Skills

Keep Moving

This is the benefit of historical experience. We know change is coming, and we are better prepared than ever before.

Put Tech on Your Side

Downside risks from further technological development can be mitigated in part by leveraging to the hilt all of the instantaneous and in-hand opportunities that we have: in-hand classroom, in-hand office, in-hand labor market, and even in-hand retail. Most people have this kind of access in the United States, and the Internet of Things will bring more people at home and abroad into the fold. This increased access should continue to create opportunities for individuals, like you.

You are Richer Than You Think

When people worry about the impact of robots and automation, it is important to keep in mind how large the wealth effect from technology has been. The greatest medieval king could not have imagined the amount of food available at any U.S. supermarket — let alone that the store might have a fully-automated checkout. And the knowledge available at anytime on your smartphone exceeds the content of everything lost in the Library of Alexandria.

There has been a growing debate about the usefulness of standard measures of the economy. In my opinion, Gross Domestic Product or GDP, is very much a good measure of how the economy is growing. But it is not a good measure of the wealth effect that technology creates.

While I was working on this book, I had a lengthy discussion about the wealth effect of technology with Louis Borders, a founder of Borders Books, Mercury Startups and HDS Global.[6] Louis pointed out to me that although wages seem to have remained stagnant, people's quality of life has gone up, because of the technology they have. After all, the average handheld device has more technology in it than the computers that launched the Apollo missions. So, if every person can own the equivalent of (what had been) a multibillion dollar computer for only a couple of hundred dollars, that really improves their quality of life. Essentially, people are wealthier in a significant and meaningful way today — even if it doesn't show up in the data. You are much richer than any of your ancestors, thanks to the technology we have. The automation age could bring you even more wealth — but only if you are prepared.

END NOTES

Introduction

1. Google Trends for Robots in the United States. Retrieved February 11, 2017: https://trends.google.com/trends/explore?date=all&geo=US&q=robots
2. Google Trends for Automation in the United States. Retrieved February 11, 2017: https://trends.google.com/trends/explore?date=all&geo=US&q=automation
3. Google Trends for Future of Work in the United States. Retrieved February 11, 2017: https://trends.google.com/trends/explore?date=all&geo=US&q=future%20of%20work
4. Google Trends for Universal Basic Income in the United States. Retrieved February 11, 2017: https://trends.google.com/trends/explore?date=all&geo=US&q=universal%20basic%20income
5. Quote sourced from Brainy Quote. Retrieved February 18, 2017: https://www.brainyquote.com/quotes/quotes/g/georgesant101521.html
6. U.S. Census Bureau. "Frequently Occurring Surnames from the Census 2000."Retrieved February 11, 2017: http://www.census.gov/topics/population/genealogy/data/2000_surnames.html
7. Appalachian Blacksmiths Association "Blacksmithing History 1." Retrieved February 11, 2017: http://www.appaltree.net/aba/hist1.htm
8. Jefferson, T. (July 2, 1776). Declaration of Independence. Retrieved from US History. Retrieved February 18, 2017: http://www.ushistory.org/DECLARATION/document/
9. Google Trends for Robots in the United States. Retrieved February 11, 2017: https://trends.google.com/trends/explore?date=all&geo=US&q=robots
10. Google Trends for Automation in the United States. Retrieved February 11, 2017: https://trends.google.com/trends/explore?date=all&geo=US&q=automation
11. Google Trends for Future of Work in the United States. Retrieved February 11, 2017: https://trends.google.com/trends/explore?date=all&geo=US&q=future%20of%20work
12. Google Trends for Universal Basic Income in the United States. Retrieved February 11, 2017: https://trends.google.com/trends/explore?date=all&geo=US&q=universal%20basic%20income

Chapter 1

1. Lohr, S. (2009, 5 Aug). "For Today's Graduate, Just One Word: Statistics." New York Times. Retrieved February 11, 2017: http://www.nytimes.com/2009/08/06/technology/06stats.html
2. Kurzweil, R. (2005). *The Singularity is Near: When Humans Transcend Biology.* New York: Penguin Books, p. 7.
3. Provided courtesy of Prestige Economics. Data from Bloomberg News.

Chapter 2

1. U.S. Census Bureau. "Frequently Occurring Surnames from the Census 2000."Retrieved February 11, 2017: http://www.census.gov/topics/population/genealogy/data/2000_surnames.html

2. Appalachian Blacksmiths Association "Blacksmithing History 1." Retrieved February 11, 2017: http://www.appaltree.net/aba/hist1.htm

3. Dolan, J.R. (1972). English Ancestral Names: The Evolution of the Surname from Medieval Occupations. New York: Crown Publishers, p. 17-18.

4. Taylor, A.J.P. (1967). *The Communist Manifesto: With an Introduction and Notes by AJP Taylor.* New York: Penguin Classics, p. 19.

5. Appalachian Blacksmiths Association "Blacksmithing History 1." Retrieved February 11, 2017: http://www.appaltree.net/aba/hist1.htm

6. Image licensed from Adobe Stock.

7. Ibid.

8. Dolan, J.R. , p. 16.

9. U.S. Bureau of Labor Statistics. "Job Openings and Labor Turnover — December 2016: Retrieved February 12, 2017: https://www.bls.gov/news.release/pdf/jolts.pdf

10. Image licensed from Adobe Stock.

11. Private photo collection of Jason Schenker.

Chapter 3

1. NBER, FRED, World Bank, Prestige Economics. Retrieved February 17, 2017:
http://www.nber.org/chapters/c1567.pdf
https://fraser.stlouisfed.org/files/docs/publications/frbslreview/rev_stls_198706.pdf
http://databank.worldbank.org/data/reports.aspx?source=world-development-indicators#

2. Ibid.

3. U.S. Bureau of Labor Statistics, All Employees: Manufacturing [MANEMP], retrieved from FRED, Federal Reserve Bank of St. Louis; https://fred.stlouisfed.org/series/MANEMP, February 18, 2017.

4. Ibid.

5. "The Most Common Job in Every State." (February 5, 2015). *NPR.* Retrieved February 11, 2017: http://www.npr.org/sections/money/2015/02/05/382664837/map-the-most-common-job-in-every-state

6. Ibid.

7. Ibid.

8. Ibid.

9. *A future that works: Automation Employment, and Productivity.* (January 2017). *McKinsey Global Institute.* McKinsey and Company, p. 4. Retrieved February 11, 2017: http://www.mckinsey.com/global-themes/digital-disruption/harnessing-automation-for-a-future-that-works

10. Ibid.

11. Ibid.

12. For more information on Solow, you can read a full lecture on Solow and the Solow growth model here: http://facstaff.uww.edu/ahmady/courses/econ302/lectures/Lecture14.pdf

13. Wolfgang, M. (September 29, 2016). "The Robotics Market – Figures and Forecasts." Presentation to Robobusiness Conference. Boston Consulting Group.

14. "Politicians cannot bring back old-fashioned factory jobs." (2017, 14 Jan). The Economist. Retrieved February 11, 2017: http://www.economist.com/news/briefing/21714330-they-dont-make-em-any-more-politicians-cannot-bring-back-old-fashioned-factory-jobs

15. U.S. Bureau of Labor Statistics as cited in Ranker.com. "The Most Common Jobs in America." Retrieved February 11, 2017:   http://www.ranker.com/list/most-common-jobs-in-america/american-jobs

16. U.S. Bureau of Labor Statistics. (December 8, 2015). "Employment Projections — 2014-24." Retrieved February 11, 2017: BLS - https://www.bls.gov/news.release/pdf/ecopro.pdf

17. U.S. Bureau of Labor Statistics. "Most New Jobs." *Occupational Outlook Handbook.* Retrieved February 11, 2017: https://www.bls.gov/ooh/most-new-jobs.htm

18. U.S. Bureau of Labor Statistics. "Fastest Growing Occupations." Occupational Outlook Handbook. Retrieved February 11, 2017: : https://www.bls.gov/ooh/fastest-growing.htm

19. U.S. Bureau of Labor Statistics. "Highest Paying Occupations." *Occupational Outlook Handbook.* Retrieved February 11, 2017: https://www.bls.gov/ooh/highest-paying.htm

Chapter 4

1. *A future that works: Automation Employment, and Productivity.* (January 2017). *McKinsey Global Institute.* McKinsey and Company, p. 5. Retrieved February 11, 2017: http://www.mckinsey.com/global-themes/digital-disruption/harnessing-automation-for-a-future-that-works

2. Ibid.

3. Ibid.

4. *Artificial Intelligence, Automation, and the Economy. Executive Office of the President* (December 20, 2016). P 16. Retrieved February 11, 2017: https://www.whitehouse.gov/sites/whitehouse.gov/files/images/EMBARGOED%20AI%20Economy%20Report.pdf

5. Ibid.

6. Ibid.

7. Ibid.

8. This entire section comes from the following: *A future that works: Automation Employment, and Productivity.* (January 2017). *McKinsey Global Institute.* McKinsey and Company, p. 21. Retrieved February 11, 2017: http://www.mckinsey.com/global-themes/digital-disruption/harnessing-automation-for-a-future-that-works

9. Ibid.

10. Gentilini, U. (January 11, 2017). "Why universal basic income is a simple, but effective idea." World Bank as reprinted by the World Economic Forum. Retrieved February 11, 2017: https://www.weforum.org/agenda/2017/01/in-a-complex-world-the-apparent-simplicity-of-universal-basic-income-is-appealing

11. Moretti, E. (2013). *The New Geography of Jobs.* New York: Mariner Books, p. 6.

12. Gentilini, U. (January 11, 2017). "Why universal basic income is a simple, but effective idea." World Bank as reprinted by the World Economic Forum. Retrieved February 11, 2017: https://www.weforum.org/agenda/2017/01/in-a-complex-world-the-apparent-simplicity-of-universal-basic-income-is-appealing

13. Keynes, J.M. (1930). "Economic Possibilities for our Grandchildren." Yale University: New Haven, p. 360. Retrieved February 11, 2017: http://www.econ.yale.edu/smith/econ116a/keynes1.pdf Please note that this quote is often incorrectly cited as coming from Keynes, J.M. *The General Theory of Employment, Interest and Money.* New York: Macmillan, 1931.

14. *Artificial Intelligence, Automation, and the Economy.* Executive Office *of* the President (December 20, 2016), p. 18. Retrieved February 11, 2017: https://www.whitehouse.gov/sites/whitehouse.gov/files/images/EMBARGOED%20AI%20Economy%20Report.pdf

15. White, J. and Ingrassia, P. (2016, 26 April) "Driverless cars could save lives, kill jobs." *Reuters.* Retrieved from: http://www.reuters.com/article/autos-driverless-winners-losers-idUSL2N17M0DO

16. *Artificial Intelligence, Automation, and the Economy.* Executive Office *of* the President (December 20, 2016), p. 18. Retrieved February 11, 2017: https://www.whitehouse.gov/sites/whitehouse.gov/files/images/EMBARGOED%20AI%20Economy%20Report.pdf

17. Kaplan, J. (2015), p. 12.

18. Ibid., p. 16.

19. Private photo collection of Jason Schenker.

20. *FinTech Survey Report* (April 2016). CFA Institute. Retrieved February 11, 2017: https://www.cfainstitute.org/Survey/fintech_survey.PDF

21. Graph capture from eSignal trading platform February 17, 2017. http://www.esignal.com/

22. United Nations. Retrieved February 11, 2017: http://www.unwater.org/water-cooperation-2013/water-cooperation/facts-and-figures/en/

23. International Energy Agency. Retrieved February 11, 2017: http://www.iea.org/topics/energypoverty/

24. United Nations. Retrieved February 11, 2017: http://www.unwater.org/water-cooperation-2013/water-cooperation/facts-and-figures/en/

25. Rodriguez, A. (March 24, 2016) "Microsoft's AI millennial chatbot became a racist jerk after less than a day on Twitter." Quartz. Retrieved February 17, 2017: https://qz.com/646825/microsofts-ai-millennial-chatbot-became-a-racist-jerk-after-less-than-a-day-on-twitter/

26. Private photo collection of Jason Schenker.

Chapter 5

1. Lerner, W. (1994). *A History of Socialism and Communism in Modern Times: Theorists, Activists, and Humanists.* Englewood Cliffs, New Jersey: Prentice Hall, p. 56.

2. *A future that works: Automation Employment, and Productivity.* (January 2017). *McKinsey Global Institute.* McKinsey and Company, p. 5. Retrieved February 11, 2017: http://www.mckinsey.com/global-themes/digital-disruption/harnessing-automation-for-a-future-that-works

3. Ibid.

4. Ibid.

5. This meme can be found online at We Know Memes. Retrieved February 11, 2017:
   http://weknowmemes.com/2013/05/the-never-ending-story-as-an-adult/

6. Kuffner, J. (September 2016). "Cloud Robotics: Intelligent Machines in a Cloud-Connected World." Presentation to Robobusiness Conference. Toyota Research Institute.

7. Kurzweil, R. (2005), p 261.

8. Schwab, K. (2016). *The Fourth Industrial Revolution.* Geneva, Switzerland: World Economic Forum, 151.

9. Private photo collection of Jason Schenker.

10. Private photo collection of Jason Schenker. Thank you Nawfal Patel, for recommending the use of Craigslist to hire a local photographer, as opposed to personally flying to Seattle to take this picture.

11. The 2015 National Retail Security Survey. (June 2015) University of Florida, p. 7. Retrieved February 17, 2017: http://users.clas.ufl.edu/rhollin/nrf%202015%20nrss_rev5.pdf

12. Ibid.

13. Waymo official press kit photos provided to Prestige Economics, LLC. February 2017.

14. "Politicians cannot bring back old-fashioned factory jobs." (2017, 14 Jan). The Economist. Retrieved February 11, 2017: http://www.economist.com/news/briefing/21714330-they-dont-make-em-any-more-politicians-cannot-bring-back-old-fashioned-factory-jobs

15. Waymo official press kit photos provided to Prestige Economics, LLC. February 2017.

16. Schwab, K. (2016), p. 147

17. U.S. Energy Information Agency. *Annual Energy Outlook 2017 (January 5, 2017)*, p. 98. Retrieved February 11, 2017: http://www.eia.gov/outlooks/aeo/pdf/0383(2017).pdf

18. U.S. Bureau of the Census, E-Commerce Retail Sales as a Percent of Total Sales [ECOMPCTSA], retrieved from FRED, Federal Reserve Bank of St. Louis; https://fred.stlouisfed.org/series/ECOMPCTSA, February 11, 2017.

19. Thank you, Kevin Vliet, for allowing me to interview you for this book.

20. Friedman, T. (2007). *The World is Flat: A Brief History of the Twenty-First Century.* New York: Picador, p. 155.

21. Ibid.

22. Kurzweil, R. (2005), p. 285.

23. Thank you, Tony Muscarello, for letting my interview you on a plane.

24. Private photo collection of Jason Schenker.

25. I ordered the cupcake, but my lovely wife, Ashley Schenker, ate the cupcake.

26. Moretti, E. (2013), p. 13.

27. Ibid.

28. Ibid.

29. Ibid.

30. Jefferson, T. (July 2, 1776). Declaration of Independence. Retrieved from US History. Retrieved February 18, 2017: http://www.ushistory.org/DECLARATION/document/

Chapter 6

1. Retrieved February 19, 2017: http://www.usdebtclock.org/

2. U.S. Department of the Treasury. Fiscal Service, Federal Debt: Total Public Debt [GFDEBTN], retrieved from FRED, Federal Reserve Bank of St. Louis; https://fred.stlouisfed.org/series/GFDEBTN, February 11, 2017.

3. Ibid.

4. Ibid.

5. Ibid.

6. Federal Reserve Bank of St. Louis and U.S. Office of Management and Budget, Federal Debt: Total Public Debt as Percent of Gross Domestic Product [GFDEGDQ188S], retrieved from FRED, Federal Reserve Bank of St. Louis; https://fred.stlouisfed.org/series/GFDEGDQ188S, February 18, 2017.

7. Desjardins, J. (August 6, 2015). "$60 Trillion of World Debt in One Visualization." Visual Capitalist. Retrieved February 11, 2017: http://www.visualcapitalist.com/60-trillion-of-world-debt-in-one-visualization/

8. Mayer, J. (November 18, 2015). "The Social Security Façade." Retrieved February 11, 2017: http://www.usnews.com/opinion/economic-intelligence/2015/11/18/social-security-and-medicare-have-morphed-into-unsustainable-entitlements

9. Image provided courtesy of The Heritage Foundation. Retrieved February 11, 2017: http://thf_media.s3.amazonaws.com/infographics/2014/10/BG-eliminate-waste-control-spending-chart-3_HIGHRES.jpg

10. Twarog, S. (January 1997). "Heights and Living Standards in Germany, 1850-1939L The Case of Wurttemberg" as reprinted in *Heath and Welfare During Industrialization.* Steckel, R. and F. Roderick Eds. Chicago: University of Chicago Press, P. 315. Retrieved February 11, 2017: http://www.nber.org/chapters/c7434.pdf

11. U.S. Social Security Administration. "Social Security History: Otto von Bismarck." Sourced from https://www.ssa.gov/history/ottob.html

12. U.S. Social Security Administration. *Fast Facts and Figures About Social Security, 8672.* Retrieved February 17, 2017: https://www.ssa.gov/policy/docs/chartbooks/fast_facts/2016/fast_facts16.pdf

13. Last, J. (2013) *What to Expect, When No One's Expecting: America's Coming Demographic Disaster.* New York: Encounter Books.,p6.

14. Bloomberg Professional Service.

15. Last (2013), p.4.

16. Ibid., p. 109.

17. Social Security Administration. Retrieved February 11, 2017 from https://www.ssa.gov/history/ratios.html Last (2013) also uses a similar table in his book on page 108.

18. Last (2013), p. 107.

19. Quartz. Interview with Bill Gates. Retrieved February 19, 2017: https://qz.com/911968/bill-gates-the-robot-that-takes-your-job-should-pay-taxes/

20. PSA Partnership for a Drug-Free America - So I can do more coke (1980). Retrieved from: http://lybio.net/tag/im-always-chasing-rainbows-psa-remarks/ https://www.youtube.com/watch?v=XGAVTwhsyOs

21. Trading Economics. Spanish youth unemployment. Retrieved February http://www.tradingeconomics.com/spain/youth-unemployment-rate

22. Trading Economics. Spanish unemployment. Retrieved February http://www.tradingeconomics.com/spain/youth-unemployment-rate

23. Washington Post. https://www.washingtonpost.com/business/capitalbusiness/minimum-wage-offensive-could-speed-arrival-of-robot-powered-restaurants/2015/08/16/35f284ea-3f6f-11e5-8d45-d815146f81fa_story.html

24. Private photo collection of Jason Schenker.

25. U.S. Internal Revenue Service. Retrieved February 19. 2017: https://www.irs.gov/businesses/small-businesses-self-employed/self-employment-tax-social-security-and-medicare-taxes

26.Pew Research Center. (October 22, 2015). Retrieved February 19, 2017: http://www.pewsocialtrends.org/2015/10/22/three-in-ten-u-s-jobs-are-held-by-the-self-employed-and-the-workers-they-hire/

27. Ibid.

Chapter 7

1. Freedman, D. (2016 July/August). "Basic Income: A Sellout of the American Dream." *MIT Technology Review*, p. 52.

2. Ibid., 53.

3. Gentilini, U. (January 11, 2017). "Why universal basic income is a simple, but effective idea." World Bank as reprinted by the World Economic Forum. Retrieved February 11, 2017: https://www.weforum.org/agenda/2017/01/in-a-complex-world-the-apparent-simplicity-of-universal-basic-income-is-appealing

4. Ibid.

5. U.S. Bureau of Labor Statistics, Consumer Price Index for All Urban Consumers: All Items [CPIAUCSL], retrieved from FRED, Federal Reserve Bank of St. Louis; https://fred.stlouisfed.org/series/CPIAUCSL, February 19, 2017.

6. Kaplan, J. (2015), 184-185.

7. Hamblin, J. (February 2, 2017) "How to Make Time Pass Quickly," *The Atlantic*: https://www.theatlantic.com/health/archive/2017/02/how-to-make-time-move/515361/

8. Thompson, D. (2015 July/August). "A World Without Work," *The Atlantic*. Retrieved from https://www.theatlantic.com/magazine/archive/2015/07/world-without-work/395294/

9. Hamblin, J. (February 2, 2017) "How to Make Time Pass Quickly," *The Atlantic*: https://www.theatlantic.com/health/archive/2017/02/how-to-make-time-move/515361/

10. Image licensed from Adobe Stock.

Chapter 8

1. Private photo collection of Jason Schenker.

2. Data on MOOCS retrieved from three sources:
   https://www.class-central.com/report/moocs-2015-stats/
   https://www.class-central.com/report/mooc-stats-2016/
   https://www.edsurge.com/news/2014-12-26-moocs-in-2014-breaking-down-the-numbers

3. Weller, C. (2016, 27 December). "A top futurist predicts the largest internet company of 2030 will be an online school." *Business Insider*. Retrieved February 17, 2017: http://www.businessinsider.com/futurist-predicts-online-school-largest-online-company-2016-12

4. Rifkin, J. (2015). *The Zero Marginal Cost Society: The Internet of Things, The Collaborative Commons, and the Eclipse of Capitalism.* New York: Palgrave Macmillan, p. 4.

5. Ibid., p. 5.

6. Private photo collection of Jason Schenker.

7. Private photo collection of Jason Schenker.

8. Private photo collection of Jason Schenker.

9. U.S. Bureau of Labor Statistics. (March 30, 2016). Occupational Employment and Wages — May 2015. Retrieved February 12, 2017: https://www.bls.gov/news.release/pdf/ocwage.pdf

10. U.S. Bureau of Labor Statistics. Retrieved February 12, 2017: https://www.bls.gov

11. Ibid.

12. Ibid.

Chapter 9

1. U.S. Bureau of Labor Statistics. (March 30, 2016). Occupational Employment and Wages — May 2015. Retrieved February 12, 2017: https://www.bls.gov/news.release/pdf/ocwage.pdf

2. Sundararajan, A. (2016). *The Sharing Economy: The End of Employment and the Rise of Crowd-Based Capitalism.* Cambridge, Massachusetts: The MIT Press, p. 177.

3. Ibid., p. 202.

4. U.S. Bureau of Labor Statistics. "Job Openings and Labor Turnover — December 2016: Retrieved February 12, 2017: https://www.bls.gov/news.release/pdf/jolts.pdf

5. Conference Board. *Help-Wanted OnLine Data Series.* Retrieved February 5[1], 645[1]: https://www.conference-board.org/data/request_form.cfm

6. Thank you, Louis Borders, for allowing me to interview you for this book.

ABOUT THE AUTHOR

Jason Schenker is the President of Prestige Economics and the world's top-ranked financial market futurist. Bloomberg News has ranked Mr. Schenker one of the most accurate forecasters in the world in 35 different categories since 2011, including #1 in the world in 20 categories for his forecasts of the Euro, the Pound, the Swiss Franc, crude oil prices, natural gas prices, gold prices, industrial metals prices, agricultural commodity prices, and U.S. non-farm payrolls.

Mr. Schenker has written three books that have been #1 Best Sellers on Amazon: *Commodity Prices 101*, *Recession-Proof*, and *Electing Recess*ion. Mr. Schenker is also a columnist for Bloomberg View and Bloomberg Prophets. Mr. Schenker has appeared as a guest and guest host on Bloomberg Television, as well as a guest on CNBC. He is frequently quoted in the press, including *The Wall Street Journal*, *The New York Times*, and *The Financial Times*.

Prior to founding Prestige Economics, Mr. Schenker worked for McKinsey & Company as a Risk Specialist, where he directed trading and risk initiatives on six continents. Before joining McKinsey, Mr. Schenker worked for Wachovia as an Economist.

Mr. Schenker holds a Master's in Applied Economics from UNC Greensboro, a Master's in Negotiation from CSU Dominguez Hills, a Master's in German from UNC Chapel Hill, and a Bachelor's with distinction in History and German from The University of Virginia. He also holds a Graduate Certificate in FinTech from MIT, a Graduate Certificate in Supply Chain Management from MIT, a Graduate Certificate in Professional Development from UNC, and a Graduate Certificate in Negotiation from Harvard Law School. Mr. Schenker holds the professional designations CMT (Chartered Market Technician), CVA® (Certified Valuation Analyst), ERP® (Energy Risk Professional), and CFP® (Certified Financial Planner).

Mr. Schenker is an active executive in FinTech, as the founder of the foreign exchange FinTech startup Hedgefly, and as a member of the Central Texas Angel Network. Previously, he was the CFO of a private equity crowdfunding startup. In October 2016, Mr. Schenker founded the Futurist Institute of America to help analysts and economists become futurists.

Mr. Schenker is a member of the Texas Business Leadership Council, the only CEO-based public policy research organization in Texas, with a limited membership of 125 CEOs and Presidents.

TOP FORECASTER ACCURACY RANKINGS

Prestige Economics, has been recognized as the most-accurate independent commodity and financial market research firm in the world. As the only forecaster for Prestige Economics, Jason Schenker is very proud that Bloomberg News has ranked him a top forecaster in 35 different categories since 2010, including #1 in the world in 20 different forecast categories.

Mr. Schenker has been top ranked as a forecaster of economic indicators, energy prices, metals prices, agricultural prices, and foreign exchange rates.

ECONOMIC TOP RANKINGS

#1 Non-Farm Payroll Forecaster in the World
#2 U.S. Unemployment Rate Forecaster in the World
#3 Durable Goods Orders Forecaster in the World
#7 ISM Manufacturing Index Forecaster in the World

ENERGY PRICE TOP RANKINGS

#1 WTI Crude Oil Price Forecaster in the World

#1 Brent Crude Oil Price Forecaster in the World

#1 Henry Hub Natural Gas Price Forecaster in the World

METALS PRICE TOP RANKINGS

#1 Gold Price Forecaster in the World

#1 Platinum Price Forecaster in the World

#1 Industrial Metals Price Forecaster in the World

#1 Copper Price Forecaster in the World

#1 Nickel Price Forecaster in the World

#1 Tin Price Forecaster in the World

#1 Zinc Price Forecaster in the World

#2 Precious Metals Price Forecaster in the World

#2 Silver Price Forecaster in the World

#2 Palladium Price Forecaster in the World

#2 Aluminum Price Forecaster in the World

#2 Lead Price Forecaster in the World

#2 Iron Ore Forecaster in the World

AGRICULTURAL PRICE TOP RANKINGS

#1 Coffee Price Forecaster in the World

#1 Cotton Price Forecaster in the World

#1 Sugar Price Forecaster in the World

#1 Soybean Price Forecaster in the World

FOREIGN EXCHANGE TOP RANKINGS

#1 Euro Forecaster in the World

#1 British Pound Forecaster in the World

#1 Swiss Franc Forecaster in the World

#1 Brazilian Real Forecaster in the World

#4 Japanese Yen Forecaster in the World

#5 Major Currency Forecaster in the World

#5 Australian Dollar Forecaster in the World

#1 EURCHF Forecaster in the World

#2 EURJPY Forecaster in the World

#2 EURGBP Forecaster in the World

#2 EURRUB Forecaster in the World

ABOUT THE PUBLISHER

Prestige Professional Publishing, LLC was founded in 2011 to produce readable, insightful, and timely professional reference books. We are registered with the Library of Congress, and we are based in Austin, Texas.

Published Titles

Be The Shredder, Not The Shred

Commodity Prices 101

Electing Recession

Jobs For Robots

Future Titles

Commodity Prices 101: Second Edition

Recession-Proof: The Futurist Edition

The Valuation Onion

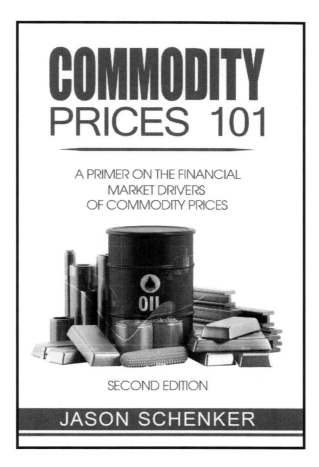

Commodity Prices 101 provides critical commodity market information to help investors, analysts, and executives meet the challenges posed by volatile commodity markets and prices. The first edition was an official #1 Best Seller on Amazon, and the second edition will be released in 2017.

Recession-Proof presents proactive strategies to help individuals survive and thrive in the next economic downturn. *Recession-Proof: The Futurist Edition* will be published by Prestige Professional Publishing in 2017. The first edition was an official #1 Best Seller on Amazon.

The Valuation Onion focuses on business valuations across industries, and how discrepancies in valuations often lead to recessions in certain industries, regions, and entire economies. *The Valuation Onion* will be published by Prestige Professional Publishing in August 2017.